Political Empowerment of Illinois' African-American State Lawmakers from 1877 to 2005

Erma Brooks Williams

UNIVERSITY PRESS OF AMERICA,® INC.
Lanham • Boulder • New York • Toronto • Plymouth, UK

University Press of America,® Inc.
4501 Forbes Boulevard
Suite 200
Lanham, Maryland 20706
UPA Acquisitions Department (301) 459-3366

Estover Road
Plymouth PL6 7PY
United Kingdom

Library of Congress Control Number: 2008924187
ISBN-13: 978-0-7618-4017-6 (clothbound : alk. paper)
ISBN-10: 0-7618-4017-6 (clothbound : alk. paper)
ISBN-13: 978-0-7618-4018-3 (paperback : alk. paper)
ISBN-10: 0-7618-4018-4 (paperback : alk. paper)

All photographs were provided by the
Illinois Secretary of State's Office.

∞™ The paper used in this publication meets the minimum
requirements of American National Standard for Information
Sciences—Permanence of Paper for Printed Library Materials,
ANSI Z39.48—1992

Contents

Introduction

African-American state legislators have a long history in the Illinois General Assembly, dating back to 1877. There is a need for their contributions and accomplishments to be known by educators, scholars, students, and the general community so that their legacy can be passed on to future generations. With this knowledge, future generations will have an understanding of the significant role of state African-American lawmakers have played in shaping public policy in Illinois and nationally.

My research relies mainly on qualitative research such as personal interviews, biographical summaries, newspaper clippings, historical journals, magazine, brochures, newsletters of the respective legislators, the internet, books, constituent correspondence, photo albums, minutes of meetings, articles of incorporation, membership directories, press releases, and video tapes.

The focus of this book provides:

- A profile of African American legislators who have and are serving in the Illinois General Assembly from 1877 to the present
- an overview of the important role that the General Assembly plays in day to day lives of the general citizenry
- a road map to the State House by these distinguished women and men
- general characteristics and geographic locations of those who made it to the State House
- highlights some of the firsts and accomplished leaders in the Illinois General Assembly
- the significant role of the Illinois Legislative Black Caucus

This book relates to other scholarly works on African American public policy makers in other states and other areas of government in the United States. This is the first comprehensive research written on this body of knowledge.

Chapter One

The Republican Era–1877 to 1943

In 1877, John W. E. Thomas became the first African American elected to the Illinois General Assembly. Between 1877 and 1943, 21 African American Republicans were elected to the Illinois General Assembly.

These distinguished gentlemen were instrumental in passing the Civil Rights Act of 1885, making Illinois the first state to enact a Civil Rights Act. Other major legislation that was introduced and supported during the Republican Era included anti slavery and lynching laws, anti-segregation measures related to Provident Hospital, legislation forbidding discrimination rates in the sale of cemetery plots, predatory and discriminatory lending and insurance practices and a myriad of other laws.

Following this Era, a small minority of African American Republicans continued to be elected from three member districts. Under cumulative voting, three Representatives were elected- at -large from within each Senatorial district. No party could nominate more than two representatives and, therefore, in many districts, a third Republican Representative was elected. Representatives Charles Gaines and Jesse Jackson were among the last of such Republican members elected. Since the enactment of single member districts in 1982, no Republican has been elected to the Illinois legislature.

John W.E. Thomas, 1877–1879; 1883–1905

John W.E. Thomas, the first African American elected to the Illinois General Assembly, was born in Montgomery, Alabama, where he was reared by a white physician and his family. He moved to Chicago after the 1863 Emancipation Proclamation, along with other Blacks who migrated to the north

John W.E. Thomas

during the first migration wave. Between 1890 and 1920, roughly 80,000 African-Americans migrated from the south between 1890 and 1920. Between 1915 and 1930, over 1.25 million relocated to the North from the south. In 1910, 75 percent of African-Americans lived in rural areas and nearly 90 percent lived in the South. By 1960, more than 75 percent lived in cities. Because of this migration, African-Americans, like Thomas, were elected to political office.

Thomas lived on the southside of Chicago and represented the Second Legislative District. He was well-known in the community by both Blacks and whites during the 1880s and 1890s due to his many civic and business ventures. Mr. Thomas owned a grocery store, practiced law, and also worked in real estate. He also established the first African American private school in Chicago.

At this time, the City of Chicago's population was approximately 400,000. The Black population was nearly 5,000, approximately two percent of the overall all municipal population. White support was necessary for Thomas to be elected. Because of his excellent reputation, Thomas gained the support he needed from the White community, including the illustrious Municipal Reform Club, of which Robert Todd Lincoln , son of President Abraham Lincoln, was a prominent member. Lincoln, however, refused to endorse Thomas's candidacy, even though Chicago newspapers branded this decision as racially motivated. White support of Mr. Thomas was significant and his election was milestone because of it.

While in the Illinois House of Representatives, Mr. Thomas sponsored the Civil Rights Act, enacted in 1885, which prohibited discrimination in public places in Illinois such as hotels, restaurants, barber shops, theatres, soda foundations, saloons, bathrooms, skating rinks, concerts, cafes, bicycle rinks, elevators, ice cream parlors, railroads and various modes of public transportation and accommodations. Violators of this law had to pay its victim a fine of $100. Illinois was the first state that enacted a state's Civil Rights Act.

George Ecton, 1887–1889

George F. Ecton, who was supported by Thomas, succeeded John W.E. Thomas in the Illinois House of Representative in 1887. A Republican, he escaped slavery in Kentucky and ended up in Ohio where he worked on the steamship that sailed the Ohio River. He moved to Chicago in 1873 and worked as a waiter in a local hotel. Mr. Ecton got involved in local politics and was later elected to the Illinois House. He introduced legislation that enforced stiffer penalities for abduction of former slaves. After serving in the legislature, he later became the owner of a baseball league.

George Ecton

Edward H. Morris, 1891–1893; 1903–1905

Edward H. Morris, an attorney, came to Chicago from Kentucky. He was born on May 30, 1855 in New York City, attended its public schools. He graduated from the City College of New York at the age of sixteen. Morris was a successful corporation lawyer, who maintained professional and social relationships with white attorneys. Morris earned the mantle of dean of African American attorneys. He was first elected to the Illinois House in 1891. Morris addressed issues related to lynching and was responsible for the School Teacher's Law. He was a founding member of the Illinois Equal Rights League. While a member of the Illinois legislature, he introduced legislation to legalize gaming in Chicago. During this era, Chicago was plagued with gambling and other criminal vices such as prostitution. This legislative

Edward H. Morris

initiative met with opposition from the "Policy King," Robert Mott. As a result, Morris lost the support of Mott, which resulted in his defeat.

John C. Buckner, 1895–1897

John C. Buckner was elected in 1895. He was born in Kendall County, Illinois on March 14, 1819. He graduated from Northwestern Illinois University in 1878 and was a professional caterer. He was affiliated with the Ninth Battalion, a combat unit, which was a part of the Illinois National Guard. Buckner was elected from the 5th District, which made up the Second, Third, Fourth and Thirty-Second Wards. He championed anti-labor violence against African-Americans. He also supported bills designed to reform existing child labor laws and welfare and led a protest of the "Spring Valley Massacre," in 1895, which was a labor conflict that left many African-American mineworkers dead.

John C. Buckner

James Bish, 1895–1897

John E. Bish was born on October 1, 1859 in Missouri to enslaved parents. He left Missouri to attend school in Belleville, Illinois, where he studied law. Bish later moved to Chicago and worked in a prominent position with Price Baking Company. Mr. Bish was also involved with real estate and served in the Illinois National Guard. Bish was the fourth African American to be elected to the Illinois General Assembly. He was the author of *Past, Present, and the Future of the Negro.* He was "one of the most prominent and influential Colored men in Chicago and prime mover in all municipal elections."

William L. Martin, 1899–1901

William L. Martin, a lawyer, was born in Missouri and was elected to the Illinois House of Representative in 1898. While in the Illinois legislature, he advanced legislation focused on preventing racial discrimination in the insurance industry. He also fought against loan predatory measures and fought for legislation that protected the rights of the disadvantaged.

John G. Jones, 1901–1903

Representative John G. Jones was an activist, lawyer, and author. He fought against segregated hospital facilities, such as Provident Hospital, which was known for training African-American nurses and doctors. While a member of the legislature, he sponsored policy brutality laws, laws against election fraud, and supported laws that provided the indigent with representation in the judicial system.

John G. Jones

Edward D. Green, 1905–1913

Representative Edward Green was born on February 25, 1865 in Pennsylvania. He later moved to St. Louis, Missouri and relocated to Chicago, Illinois and where he became active in Republican politics. In 1904, he was the only African-American serving in the Illinois General Assembly. While a member, he secured passage of an amendment to the Civil Rights Law forbidding discriminatory rates in the sale of cemetery plots.

Edward D. Green

Alexander Lane, 1907–1911

Alexander Lane was born on October 26, 1857 in Lexington, Mississippi. Like many African-American families, his family migrated to the north by settling in southern Illinois. He attended Southern Illinois University Normal School, where he studied to be an educator. He served as principal of a local school. In 1905, he graduated from Rush Medical College as a dentist. While serving as a member of the legislature, he represented the 1st District.

Robert R. Jackson, 1912–1919

Representative Robert R. Jackson, a Republican, was born in 1870 in Chicago. He left school in the eighth grade to work successively as a newsboy, bootblack, and postal worker. He finally established a publishing and printing business. He was a member of social lodges, such as the Knights of Pythias, which he found useful bases for political support. He later served as alderman of the 2nd and 3rd Wards.

Sheadrick B. Turner, 1915–1917; 1919–1929

Representative Turner, a lawyer and a Republican, was the publisher of *The State Capital and Illinois Idea* newspapers. He moved his newspaper from Springfield, Illinois to Chicago, and used it as a personal organ that eventually helped him win a seat in the Illinois House. While a member of the House, he introduced legislation to discourage the organization of the Klu Klux Klan. He also sponsored an appropriation bill to provide $35,000 for the investigation of bomb throwing.

Benjamin H. Lucas, 1917–1919

Benjamin H. Lucas, a Republican, was born on July 4, 1879 in Brooklyn, Illinois. He was a postal office worker and later worked in the insurance industry. Representative Lucas was affiliated with the Masons and served as the State Grand Marshall of the United Brothers of Friendships. He was elected to the Illinois House of Representatives in 1916.

Warren B. Douglas, 1919–1923; 1925–1929

Warrem B. Douglas was born on January 25, 1886 in Fayette, Missouri. He graduated from Western University in Quindaro, Kansas. After graduating from the university, he attended Chicago-Kent School of Law and began in local politics under the leadership of Congressman Oscal DePriest, although he aligned himself with the opposing faction of the prominent African-American congressman. Douglas served in the Illinois House from 1919 to 1929.

Warren B. Douglas

His major contribution was legislation to name streets, parks, or driveways in memory of Jean Pointe DuSable. He was reelected to office in 1934, but died before assuming office for that term.

George T. Kersey, 1923–1925; 1927–1931

George T. Kersey, a Republican, was born in North Carolina and later migrated with his family to Chicago. He was a mortician and served as director of the Douglass National Bank, the first black-owned bank in the United States. He was a member of the Masons, the Odd Fellows, the Elks and the Knights of Pythias. Representative Kersey was elected to the Illinois House, representing the Third Legislative District. Kersey's major contribution was that he introduced legislation that provided for a committee to investigate the action of the Chicago Police Department for making an usually large number of arrests of African-American voters in the city of Chicago.

George T. Kersey

Adelbert H. Roberts, 1924–1935

The Great Migration of World War I years brought about an on-going migration of Blacks coming from the South to the North to escape Jim Crow and segregation. As migration continued in the 1920's, urban African-American communities grew in size, which resulted in the organization of new institutions and allocation of new resources. African-Americans responded with new cultural and political energy. This gave African-Americans an opportunity to elect an African-American to the Illinois State Senate fifty-years a after Thomas was elected to the Illinois House of Representatives. Roberts, who as a prominent attorney and Republican, became the first African-African to be elected to t he Illinois State Senate.

Adelbert H. Roberts

William E. King, 1925–1939

William King was elected to the Illinois House in 1925. He was born on May 12, 1885 in Louisiana. He matriculated at Philander-Smith College in Little Rock, Arkansas. He attended John Marshall School of Law. He was mentored by Oscar De Priest. He is credited for legislation to abolish the Ku Klux Klan (KKK).

William E. King

Charles A. Griffin, 1925–1929

Charles A. Griffin, a Republican, was born on January 24, 1884 in Bellaire, Ohio. He migrated to Chicago, Illinois after graduating from high school. He was a real estate and insurance broker. He was elected to the Illinois House, representing the First District. Griffin introduced anti-discrimination laws related to admission to college, university and high school. He was the founder of the Metropolitan Community Center and co-founder of the Wabash YMCA, the first YMCA that was available for African-Americans. He was a member of the Elks, the Masons, and the Foresters.

George W. Blackwell, 1929–1933

George W. Blackwell was born in Richmond, Virginia. He attended Tuskegee University and later graduated from Howard University Law School in 1910. He moved to Chicago and served as an assistant attorney for the City of Chicago. In 1928, he was elected as a Republican to the Illinois House, representing the First Legislative District. As a member of the legislature, he championed laws related to the real estate industry.

George W. Blackwell

Harris B. Gaines, 1929–1937

Harris B. Gaines was born in Henderson, Kentucky and later migrated to Chicago, Illinois with his family. He attended DePaul University, John Marshall Law School and the University of Chicago. He worked for the law firm of Ellis and Westbrooks and worked as an assistant attorney He was elected to the Illinois House in 1928. Gaines was a strong advocate of civil rights and unemployment legislation. He too was an assistant state's attorney. Gaines was very active with the fraternal orders.

WILLIAM J. WARFIELD, 1929–1945

William J. Warfield was born in Chicago, Illinois. He was a real estate broker and worked with the Board of Assessors of Cook County as a tax expert af-

Harris B. Gaines

ter serving in the U.S. Army. After receiving the support of prominent political leader Oscar DePriest, he ran for the Illinois House of Representatives in 1928 and represented the Fifth District in Chicago. Warfield sponsored legislation related to cemetery associations, horse racing and real estate. He was actively involved with the Masons.

William J. Warfield

Charles J. Jenkins, 1931–1955

Charles J. Jenkins was born on October 4, 1897 in Austin, Texas. He later moved to Chicago with his family. He attended Wendell Phillips High School in 1914. After graduating from Wendell Phillips, he returned to Texas and attended Bishop College in Marshall, Texas. He then moved back to Chicago and attended Chicago-Kent College of Law. He later served as an Assistant Corporation Counsel for the City of Chicago in 1928. Jenkins was elected to the Illinois House of Representatives in 1930 and served until 1955. As a

Charles J. Jenkins

legislator, he introduced legislation to amend the Riot Act that provided $10,000 to any person injured by mob action while on public property. He also sponsored legislation that provided $3,000 for the erection of a statute in memory of soldiers who lost their lives in WWI. He also championed the passage of the equal opportunity legislation in the House; however, it failed in the Illinois Senate. Jenkins was the first African American to chair the powerful House Appropriations Committee.

Earnest A. Greene, 1937–1943; 1955–1957

Earnest A. Greene, a Republican, was born in Rome, Georgia. He graduated from Talladega College in Alabama and completed graduate studies in law at Chicago-Kent College of Law. He was elected to the Illinois House in 1936. He sponsored legislation that would prevent any union that practiced racial

Earnest A. Greene

discrimination from being part of collective bargaining. He also sponsored the State Fair Employment Practices legislation that prohibited discrimination in employment in state agencies, which was unsuccessful.

J. Horace Gardner, 1957–1965; 1967–1972

J. Horace Gardner was born in Cairo, Illinois. In 1948, he was elected Committeeman of the 20th Ward.

Robert Holloway, 1973–1975

Robert Holloway was born on May 4, 1918 in Arkansas. He served in World War II, rising to the rank of Captain. Holloway earned his law degree from Loyola University. He then worked as an Assistant State's Attorney and was elected to the Illinois House in 1972 for one term.

Chapter Two

Democratic Era—1943 to Present

During the Hebert Hoover's Administration, many African Americans were faced with many social ills ranging from unemployment to homelessness. Because of the failure of the Republican Party to address these concerns, African Americans switched their party loyalty to Franklin Roosevelt, embracing the principles of the Democratic Party and the New Deal philosophy. African Americans in Chicago followed the leadership of Congressman William L. Dawson, formerly a loyal Republican, crossed over to the Democratic Party. Backed by strong ward organizations in the Second and Third Wards, Democrats sent Senator Fred Smith, Dean of the Senate, and Representative Cornell (Deacon) Davis to Springfield.

During the 40's, 50's and 60's, a steady flow of African American Democrats were elected to the General Assembly from the South and West Side of Chicago. They were party loyalists. However, they continued to press for changes important to the Black community.

Aubrey H. Smith, 1935–1937

Representative Smith was the first Democrat to be elected to the Illinois General Assembly from East St. Louis, Illinois, graduated from Fisk University and matriculated from Northwestern University Dental School. He relocated to East St. Louis and became involved with politics. He was elected for one term to the Illinois General Assembly. While a member of the General Assembly, his major contributions included introducing laws related to civil rights related to rest rooms on motor vehicle lines. He pushed for laws that

Aubrey H. Smith

would provide that restrooms be made available at 50 mile interval on public transportation lines.

Richard A. Harewood, 1937–1939; 1957–1959

Richard A. Harewood was born on June 25, 1900 in Barbados, British West Indies. When he was young, his family moved to Chicago. He attended the University of Illinois at Urbana-Champaign in 1922. In 1926, he graduated from the University of Chicago Law School. He served as Assistant State's Attorney of Cook County and Assistant Corporation Counsel for the City of Chicago. He was elected to the Illinois House as a Republican in 1936 and later as a Democrat in 1956. His major contributions included civil rights legislation related to employment discrimination, mob violence, school discrimination and segregation and the establishment of the University of Illinois at Chicago campus.

Richard A. Harewood

William A. Wallace, 1939–1943

William A. Wallace, a Democrat, was born on June 6, 1867 in Maryland. He graduated from Lincoln University in Pennsylvania. He moved to Chicago and later was elected to the Illinois Senate in 1938. Wallace championed anti-discrimination legislation related to schools, housing and public utilities.

William A. Wallace

Andrew A. Torrence, 1939–1940

Andrew A. Torrence was born on June 8, 1902 in Baltimore, Maryland. He graduated from the University of Detroit. He later graduated from Northwestern University School of Law. He was elected to the Illinois House in 1938.

Andrew A. Torrence

Dudley S. Martin, 1941–1943

Dudley S. Martin, a Republican, was born on November 18, 1903 in Forest Hill, Tennessee. After graduating from LeMoyne College, he moved to Chicago, Illinois. He became active in local politics in the Second Ward Regular Republican organization. He was elected to the Illinois House in 1940, representing the Third District. He passed legislation that enabled welfare recipients to be insured by policies in the amount of $500. He also championed legislation that addressed discrimination of African-American serving in the military.

Dudley S. Martin

Fred J. Smith, 1943–1955; 1955–1979

Senator Fred J. Smith, was born on April 14, 1892 in small town called Kosse, Texas on a big farm consisting of 487 acres. Both his parents were slaves. He came to Chicago during the first Great Migration. Republican Big Bill Thompson was the Mayor of Chicago during that time. He worked for the Illinois Central Railroad and for the Pennsylvania Railroad and Continental National Bank until he retired in 1979. Senator Smith was elected to the Illinois House of Representatives for twelve years and served in the Illinois State Senate from 1953 until 1979. He married Senator Margaret Smith. While a member of the Illinois General Assembly, Senator Smith, an independent, championed civil rights, employment rights, anti-school segregation and collective bargaining legislation for African-Americans. Because he worked for the railroad industry, he sponsored legislation related to railroads.

According to the late Senator Margaret Smith in an interview shortly before her death, her husband, Fred, mentored the late mayor Harold Washington while he served in the Illinois legislature.

Fred J. Smith

Christopher C. Wimbush, 1943–1955

Christopher C. Wimbush was born in Atlanta, Georgia in 1895. He earned his Bachelor's degree from Howard University and a law degree from Northwestern University. Like most African-Americans who claimed up the political ladder, he served as an Assistant Corporation Counsel for the City of Chicago. In 1942, he successfully was elected to the Illinois State Senate. Like his predecessor, Corneal A. Davis, he fought and secured equal pay for teachers in the Cairo, Illinois school system.

Christopher C. Wimbush

Corneal A. Davis, 1943–1979

Corneal A. Davis, who was known as the Dean of Senate and Deacon Davis, served twenty-seven years in the Illinois House of Representatives from 1943

Corneal A. Davis

to 1979. He was the first African-American to serve as Assistant Minority Leader in the Illinois General Assembly in 1971. At that time, he was the longest serving member of the Illinois General Assembly. He was born in rural Mississippi in 1900 to a white landowner and an African-American ex-slave mother. After his graduation from high school, his father offered to pay all his expenses if he would go to an eastern white university and not disclose his African heritage. Corneal refused that offer, saying that he would never deny or insult his mother in that way. He, instead, attended Alcorn A & M College, where he met many other African-American students of mixed descent. He came to Chicago in 1919 during the race riot. He got involved in politics early under the Republican leadership of Second Ward Alderman Oscar DePriest. He, like other African-Americans, shifted their party affiliation from the Republican Party to the Democratic Party in 1936. Representative Davis was a very outspoken, articulate and effective defender of civil rights for African-Americans.

While serving in the Illinois House, he served as the Assistant Majority Leader, served as chair of the House Public Aid Health, Welfare and Safety Committee. He is known for his success in stopping the University of Illinois budget until the university agreed to admit more African-Americans to its medical school. His strategy was effective because this bill's purpose was to provide appropriations for the University of Illinois to establish the Chicago campus. Davis knew that this was a critical time to push for more African-American medical students. Otherwise, he might not have ever gotten the opportunity once the University had secured its appropriations from the General Assembly. Representative Davis also fought for pay equity for African-American teachers in Cairo, Illinois. He also helped to pass legislation that made it illegal to discriminate in employment in Illinois. The result was the establishment of the Illinois Fair Employment Practice Commission.

Charles M. Skyles

Charles M. Skyles, 1945–1957

Representative Charles M. Skyles was born in 1905 in Little Rock, Arkansas. Like many other African-Americans, he migrated with his family to Chicago, Illinois. He graduated from Wendell Phillips High School and attended Garret Seminary at Northwestern University. He was an ordained Methodist minister and was assigned to congregations in Davenport, Iowa and Winnipeg, Manitoba. He pursued graduate studies at the University of Toronto. He later returned to Chicago and attended John Marshall Law School. After completing law school, he held various posts in City government and was also the owner of a barbershop. Representative Skyles was elected to the Illinois House in 1944. While a member of the Illinois General Assembly, he fought against discriminatory laws affecting African-Americans. He also was a cosponsor of the bill to establish the Fair Employment Practice Act. Skyles also supported workmen's and unemployment compensation legislation as well as wrongful imprisonment, minimum wage standards and funding for public assistance recipients. He was also an advocate for teachers. He sponsored the teachers' pension act. Skyles was married to the former Mildred Thomas. They had four children, Dolores, Ruby, Charles Jr. and Ethel, who later was elected to the Illinois House, following her father's footsteps.

James Y. Carter, 1955–1973

James Y. Carter , a Democrat, was born on April 20, 1915 in Raleigh, North Carolina. He earned his Bachelor's Degree from Hampton. He later earned a Master's Degree and Law Degree from Boston University. He was a member of the renowned Tuskegee Airmen. Before serving in the Illinois legislature, he held various positions with the City of Chicago. Carter was elected to the Illinois House in 1954. As a member of the Illinois General Assembly, he championed civil rights and employment discrimination measures.

Elwood Graham, 1957–1965; 1967–1973

Elwood Graham was born in Chicago, Illinois in the early 1900's. He served in World War I and held various public service jobs. Later, he became a real estate broker and worked for the DuSable Realty Company. He was involved in the 6th Ward Regular Democratic Organization and was elected to the Illinois House in 1956. As a member of the House, he supported laws prohibiting employment discrimination, bombing of property, and mob violence. He too supported the teachers pension law.

Charles F. Armstrong, 1957–1965

Charles F. Armstrong, a Democrat, was born on May 25, 1919 in Statesville, North Carolina. He graduated from Tuskegee Institute. After serving in World War II, he moved to Chicago, Illinois and attended John Marshall Law School. After holding several public service jobs, including Assistant State's Attorney for Cook County, he was elected to the Illinois House in 1965. While serving as a member of the House, he introduced legislation addressing the school system redistricting, civil rights, employment discrimination, establishment of the Fair Employment Practice Commission and anti-mob violence.

Charles F. Armstrong

Kenneth E. Wilson

Kenneth E. Wilson, 1955–1965

Kenneth E. Wilson was born on September 24, 1919 in Tacoma, Washington. He completed his undergraduate studies at Hampton University. He earned a Juris Doctorate Degree from the University of Chicago Law School and was admitted to the Illinois Bar. The distinguished Wilson was appointed as Assistant Attorney General, serving until 1952. Later, he was hired as a Cook County Assistant State's Attorney. His distinguished legal career helped land him a seat in the Illinois House of Representatives in 1954 for 10 years. After his service in the Illinois legislature, he later served as an Appellate Court judge in Cook County.

William H. Robinson, 1955–1965

William H. Robinson was born on May 1, 1909 in Virginia. He earned his Bachelor's Degree from Virginia Union University and later moved to Chicago and earned his degree in the School of Social Service Administration at the University of Chicago. He served in World War II and later returned to Chicago and worked in various social service venues. He was elected to the Illinois House in 1954. While a member of the Illinois General Assembly, he sponsored anti-mob and, civil rights legislation in housing, workmen's compensation and occupational disease legislation. After his service in the Illinois legislature, he later became Chairman of the Chicago Urban League's Board. The Robinson Building at Chicago State University was named in his honor.

Floy Clements, 1959–1961

In 1958, Floy Clements, a Democrat, was the first African-American female elected to the Illinois House of Representatives, representing the 22nd

William H. Robinson

District on the Southside of Chicago. She was born in Memphis, Tennessee, November 20, 1909. Ms. Clements graduated from Wilberforce University. She served as a precinct captain in the Fourth Ward Regular Democratic Organization for more than twenty years and was committeewoman for several years. While serving in the Illinois House of Representatives, she championed juvenile and criminal justice measures, transportation and utilities legislation. She was a member of St. Mark Methodist Church in the middle class Chatham-Avalon community.

Cecil A. Partee, 1957–1977

The son of a school teacher, Cecil A. Partee, a Democrat, served in the Illinois House of Representatives from 1957–1967 and from 1976–1977 in the Illinois State Senate. He was tapped by William Dawson to run for the Illi-

Cecil A. Partee

nois House of Representatives on the Southside of Chicago, representing the 22 Legislative District. He was the Vice-President of the 20th Ward Regular Democratic Organization. Prior to this time, Blacks were members of the Republican Party when Hebert Hoover, a conservative Republican, was President; however, during the Depression around 1933, they became dissatisfied with the Republican Party because they suffered from high unemployment, homelessness and many other social ills, broke from the Republican Party during President Roosevelt New Deal. Roosevelt offered more than Republicans did. Blacks followed the lead of William Dawson, who was a Republican, switched their loyalty from the Republicans to the Democratic Party. Partee was one of the benefactors of this political change. He was very loyal to the Democratic Machine. Although he was loyal to the Machine, he also looked out for the interest of the Black community. Thus, while serving in the Illinois General Assembly, he championed the establishment of the Fair Employment Practice Commission. He was the first African-American legislator to serve as one of the state's top four legislative leaders, both as the Senate Minority Leader, and later, as the first African-American Senate President. He made major contributions to the evolution of Black political empowerment in both Chicago and across the State of Illinois.

He came to Chicago in the 1940's as part of the Black Migration. He attended Northwestern University Law School because Jim Crow Laws did not allow him to attend law school in the state of Arkansas. When he graduated from Tennessee State University in Nashville, Tennessee, he applied for admission to the University of Arkansas Law School. He passed the admission test, but that law school was all white, so the State of Arkansas told Cecil Partee that they would pay his tuition for any law school he could be admitted to outside of the State of Arkansas. It turned out that he was admitted to Northwestern University Law School in Chicago. Arkansas' loss was Illinois' gain. Senator Partee graduated from Northwestern Law School and was admitted to the bar in Illinois. He completed law school in a record time of two years. He was a brilliant man.

Senator Partee championed important legislation such as the Illinois Housing Act and, he along with the late Mayor Harold Washington and other members of the Illinois Legislative Black Caucus, passed legislation making Martin Luther King a state Holiday in Illinois. On several occasions, he was voted "Best Freshman Senator" in the mid-sixties. He also fought for consumer rights, civil rights, crime and correction legislation, judicial and fiscal reform, open housing legislation, and public aid and welfare issues.

After leaving the Illinois State Senate, he was the first African-American to run for a statewide office, the Illinois Attorney General, in 1976. It is believed that he was encouraged to run for the Illinois Attorney General Office so that he could give up the powerful President of the Senate post. Mr. Partee was elected as Cook County first African-American State's Attorney in 1989. He was also the first Chicago City Treasurer. Mr. Partee passed in 1996.

Lycurgus J. Conner, 1961–1965

Lycurgus J. Conner, a Democrat, was born on November 17, 1909 in Chicago, Illinois. He was a graduate of Hyde Park High School. He earned his Bachelor's Degree from the University of Chicago as well as his doctorate of juris prudence. He too served in World War II. He was elected to the Illinois House in 1960 and served until his death in 1965. Conner's major contributions were penalty for violations of civil rights, creation of police boards for cities with population of 500,000 or more, elimination of segregation in schools, the establishment of the engineering program at Southern Illinois University and unemployment compensation legislation.

Harold Washington, 1965–1980

Harold Washington was sworn in as a legislator in the Illinois House of Representatives on January 6, 1965. He was elected by the Machine and later broke with the Machine when he was confronted with voting for issues that were in the best interest of African-Americans. He served in the Illinois House of Representatives through 1977. He was elected to the Illinois Senate in 1977 and served until 1980. He then went on to serve in the U.S. House of Representatives from 1981 to 1983. In 1983, he was elected as the first African-American Mayor of the City of Chicago.

Harold Washington

While serving in the Illinois legislature, he voted for the establishment of the Fair Employment Practice Commission, along with the late Senators Richard Newhouse of Hyde Park, Fred Smith, Kenneth Hall, and Charles Chew and Representatives Ray Ewell, Lewis A.H. Caldwell, and Corneal Davis. He also supported the Equal Rights Amendment and the creation of the Fair Housing Act. He opposed state aid for parents sending their children to private and parochial schools and supported an annual cost-of-living review for public aid recipients. He successfully pushed a large number of consumer protection measures. Washington in 1969, along with Caldwell, Ewell, Newhouse, Smith, and Hall recognized the power of working together, organized the Illinois Legislative Black Caucus. He also introduced a bill to establish a statewide holiday in honor of Martin Luther King, Jr.'s birthday and the establishment of the Illinois Human Rights Commission. In 1977, Washington was voted as "One of the Ten Best Legislators in the State of Illinois." While serving as a member of Congress in 1981, he led the successful fight for extension of the Voting Rights Act.

Born in 1922, he earned his high school equivalency diploma in the U.S. Army. Later, he attended Roosevelt University and Northwestern University's Law School.

Calvin Smith, 1965–1969

Calvin Smith,a Democrat, was born in Springfield, Illinois. He later moved to Chicago, Illinois with his family. He graduated from the University of Illinois at Urbana-Champaign in 1930 from the School of Pharmacy. He owned a pharmacy with his father. He served as President of the Pharmaceutical Association from 1951 to 1952. He later became active in the 4th Ward Democratic Organization. He was elected to the Illinois House in 1964. Smith's most important contributions as a legislator were supporting legislation related to teacher work load compensation and passage of legislation to establish apprentice programs for African-American students.

Melvin McNairy, 1965–1967

Melvin McNairy, a Democrat, was born on October 2, 1910. He was educated in the Catholic schools in Chicago. He later served in World War II. He was an executive in the insurance industry, where he served as Vice-President of Chicago Metropolitan Mutual Assurance Company. He later became active in politics where he served as Alderman of the 21st Ward. In 1964, he was elected to the Illinois House of Representatives.

Melvin McNairy

OTIS G. COLLINS, 1965-1973

Otis Collins, a Democrat, was born on May 2, 1917 in Camden, Mississippi. He migrated to Detroit, Michigan and later to Gary, Indiana, before moving to Chicago, Illinois. He graduated from Wendell Phillips High School and later attended Wilson Junior College. He earned his Business Degree from Northwestern University. After serving in WWII, he matriculated to Roosevelt University and studied real estate. He also was active in the labor movement, where he served as Chairman of Local Union Delegates in the Chicago CIO Industrial Union Council. In 1964, he was elected to the Illinois House. While a member of the House, he supported criminal justice, police reform, repeal of the Stop and Frisk Law, welfare reform, establishment of the Fair Employment Practice Commission, and programs for pre-apprenticeship in high schools for African-American students. He was married to Earlean Collins, who assumed his seat after death.

PAUL P. BOSWELL, 1965-1967

Paul P. Boswell, a Republican, was born on June 12, 1905 in Pittsburgh, Pennsylvania. He migrated to Minneapolis, Minnesota with his family. He later attended Lincoln University in Pennsylvania and later graduated from the University of Minnesota Medical School. He did his internship at Provident Hospital. He was a professor of medicine at the University of Illinois-Champaign Medical School. Boswell was elected to the Illinois House in 1964 and served for one term. He was active with various medical associations, the Urban League and his fraternity organization.

Owen D. Pelt

Owen D. Pelt, 1967–1969

Owen D. Pelt was born near Jackson, Mississippi, on April 23, 1916. He attended Natchez College and Jackson College. He migrated to Chicago, Illinois and attended the University of Chicago Divinity School. After matriculating at the University of Chicago, he returned to Mississippi and entered the ministry. He later moved back to Illinois and resided in Centralia, where he became the pastor of Second Baptist Church. He later moved back to Chicago and became the pastor of the renowned Shiloh Baptist Church in Chicago, Illinois. In 1966, he was elected to the Illinois of Representatives. Pelt's major contribution were legislation to create the Fair Employment Practice Commission term of office, and an appropriation to create the Police Relations Commission to study problems of police in their relationship with minority groups.

Isaac R. Sims, 1967–1975

Isaac R. Sims was born on February 14, 1914. He graduated from McKinley High School and Northwestern School of Commerce. He was an entrepreneur. He owned a grocery store and later the insurance business where he founded the Freedom Insurance Corporation. He was elected to the Illinois House of Representatives in 1966. Sims' major contributions included support of the Fair Employment Practice Commission and legislation related to real estate, insurance and motor vehicle and traffic regulations.

Raymond W. Ewell, 1967–1963

Raymond W. Ewell was born on December 29, 1928 in Chicago, Illinois. He graduated from Englewood High School in Chicago. He earned his Bachelor's Degree in History from the University of Illinois and a Masters Degree in History Education. Ewell later graduated from the University of Chicago Law School. He later became active in the 4th Ward Young Democratic Organization. He served in the military. After his service in the army, he operated a gas station and later practiced law. He was a partner in the firm of Ewell, Graham, McCormick, Ross and Davidson. Ewell was elected to the Illinois legislature in 1967 and he, along with other progressive African-Americans in the Illinois General Assembly, organized the Illinois Legislative Black Caucus. Ewell championed legislation that advanced the plight of African-Americans, such as equal employment and fair housing.

Charles Chew, Jr., 1967–1986

Charles Chew, Jr., was born on October 9, 1922 in Greenville, Mississippi. He earned his undergraduate Business Administration degree from Tuskegee Institute in Alabama in 1942. He served in World War II. Chew moved to Chicago after the army and held various high level administrative positions such as Vice-President of Jackson Mutual Life Insurance Company, Vice President of Chew Brothers Building Company and President of South Parkway Safe Deposit Corporation. He also wrote a newspaper column. Chew later became involved in politics where he was elected to the City Council from 1963 to 1967. In 1966, he was elected to the Illinois State Senate, representing the 29th Legislative District. As a progressive legislator, he was one of the co-founders of the Illinois Legislative Black Caucus, where he fought diligently for civil rights legislation. He also served as the vice-chair of the Transportation Committee. He championed traffic safety legislation, consumer fraud, credit reform, education opportunity and employment, fair housing and other major legislation. Chew sponsored the legislation to make 55 mph speed limit permanent. In 1986, Ethel Skyles Alexander succeeded him in the Illinois Senate.

Richard H. Newhouse, 1967–1991

Senator Richard Newhouse was elected to the Illinois State Senate in 1966, representing the 24th Legislative District. As a member of the Illinois Gen-

Richard H. Newhouse

eral Assembly, he along with Harold Washington, Lewis A. H. Caldwell, Richard Newhouse, Raymond Ewell, Charles Chew, and others founded the Illinois Legislative Black Caucus. Newhouse supported legislation related to capital expenditures for the establishment of Kennedy-King college, repeal of the Stop and Frisk Law, establishment of the Fair Employment Practice Commission, establishment of the Illinois Fair Housing Practices Act, school funding, juvenile justice legislation, as well as special education laws. This was likely because his son had some special needs. In 1982, Newhouse was the founder of the Newhouse Architectural Competition for Chicago Public School students. His goal was to encourage and nurture African American students who expressed an interest in art and design. He also fought for African American hiring on state capital construction projects such as Washburn Trade School and the McCormick Place expansion. His activism paved the way for future lawmakers such as former Representative Charles Morrow who fought fiercely for African American participation on the Dan Ryan Expressway expansion.

Senator Newhouse was born in Louisville, Kentucky on January 24, 1924. He served in World War II. After his service in the military, he graduated from Boston University with a degree in Journalism and earned his Master's of Arts Degree in 1951. In 1961, he graduated from the University of Chicago Law School. He resided in Hyde Park.

Genoa Washington, 1967–1972

Genoa Washington was born in Washington, D.C. He earned his Bachelor's Degree and law degree from Northwestern University. He became the first

Genoa Washington

Vice-President of the Cook County Bar Association. Washington was appointed by President Dwight D. Eisenhower as a delegate to the 12th General Assembly of the United Nations. He was elected to the Illinois House in 1966. Washington championed civil rights laws and women rights legislation,

Lewis A. H. Caldwell, 1969–1979

Representative Caldwell, a Democrat, served in the Illinois House of Representatives from 1969 to 1979. He was a member of the Chicago Urban League and he is the founder of the Cosmopolitan Chamber of Commerce, which was established to assist African-American business development because they could not become members of the mainstream chamber of commerce. He also ran the operations of Baldwin Ice Cream. Mr. Caldwell, in the 1940s, wrote his master's thesis at Northwestern University, on Policy, which was known as "the numbers", which is what is known as the lottery today. At that time, this

Lewis A. H. Caldwell

illegal activity was ran by Robert Motts and was the economic base of the African-American community that helped finance education and other economic development activities in the community, grossed approximately $10 million annually. Motts was endeared by the community because he employed many African-Americans who was unable to secure traditional employment. When the mob recognized the amount of money that Policy brought into the community, they took control. In the 1970s, Mr. Caldwell ran for state representative and won. He introduced the Policy Numbers Game Act to legalize Policy as a lottery game. The profits to be gained by this legislation would legalize Policy as a lottery game. The proceeds would be used to fund education. The legislation passed; however, the money was never used solely for education but was diverted to the General Revenue Fund (GRF).

Robert L. Thompson, 1969–1974

Robert L. Thompson, a Democrat, was born in Louisiana. He migrated to Chicago, Illinois in 1920. He was a firefighter and was president of Thompson Insurance Agency. Thompson was elected to the Illinois House in 1968, representing the 13th Legislative District, which included the Cabrini-Green housing development. He too was a founding member of the Illinois Legislative Black Caucus. Thompson's contributions were related to school funding equalization, real estate, water works, zoning and motor vehicle legislation.

James A. McLendon, 1969–1983

Senator McClendon earned his Bachelor's Degree from Fisk University and a Juris Doctorate Degree from Northwestern University. He enlisted in the

James A. McLendon

U.S. Army during World War II, serving on the staff of the Judge Advocate General of the Army and rising to the rank of Lieutenant Colonel. McClendon served as Master of Chancery for the Superior Court of Cook County, an arbitrator for the Industrial Commission of Illinois and staff Attorney for the Chicago Transit Authority. He was elected to the Illinois House from 1965 to 1976 and 1969 to 1979 and was elected to the Illinois Senate from 1979 to 1983.

Eugene M. Barnes, 1970–1980

Eugene M. Barnes was elected to the Illinois House of Representatives in 1970. He was born in Chicago, Illinois and grew up in the Chatham community. He was one of ten children. Mr. Barnes became engaged in local politics under the leadership of the late Ralph Metcalfe with his mother and father, who were active in the William Dawson's political organization. He was also active in the 8th Ward Democratic Organization. As a legislator, he was chairman of the Appropriations II Committee and was active in a number of other legislative areas. While a member of the Illinois House, as chairman of the Appropriations Committee, he was the co-sponsor of the first Illinois lottery legislation, along with Lewis A.H. Caldwell. He also was the original sponsor of the sickle cell anemia legislation, which provided funding for this disease that affect African-Americans disportionately. Illinois was the first state to provide funding for this kind of health initiative. Mr. Barnes championed education. He awarded numerous legislative scholarships to students to pursue medical school. He also sponsored legislation to stipulate that after medical students graduated from medical school in Illinois, they would be re-

Eugene M. Barnes

quired to practice in underserved areas. As chairman of the Appropriations Committee, he secured funding for the original buildings at Chicago State University campus on 95th and Martin Luther King Drive, in Chicago, Illinois. He also secured funding for the library's acquisitions. He was one of the original founders of the Illinois Legislative Black Caucus.

In 1983, Mr. Barnes was named Commissioner of the Department of Sewers for the City of Chicago, under the late mayor Harold Washington. Prior to that appointment, he served as an administrative assistant to Mayor Washington and as a legislative fiscal analyst for the Chicago City Council Finance Committee. Mr. Barnes served as the first African-American chairman of the Chicago Transit Authority. As chairman of the transit authority, he persuaded CTA to invest in African-American banks for the first time in its history. Seaway National Bank was one of the recipients of this initiative.

Mr. Barnes is CEO of E.M. Barnes & Associates, an independent lobbying firm. Prior to that, he was a partner with Cook Witter, Incorporated, in 1986. He also served as a member of the Illinois Pension Laws Commission.

Peggy Smith Martin, 1973–1974; 1977–1979

Peggy Smith Martin, an Independent, was born on May 22, 1931 in Corinth, Mississippi. After living in several cities throughout the United States, her family moved to Chicago, where she earned her Bachelors Degree from Governor's State University in Correctional and Criminal Justice. She got involved in politics and was later elected to the Illinois House in 1972 as the second African-American female. Martin was recognized by the Independent Voters of Illinois as "Best Legislator."

Peggy Smith Martin

Langdon W. Patrick, 1973–1977; 1979–1981

Langdon W. Patrick, a Democrat, was born on April 11, 1914 in Lynchburg, Virginia and later migrated to Chicago, Illinois. He worked for Greyhound Bus Lines and later for Pullman Company. He served in the U.S. Army. After service to the military, he returned to Chicago and worked in various county and municipal positions. He was elected to the Illinois House in 1972. He was active in the 29th Ward Democratic Organization. Patrick advanced legislation related to local government and the law that provides that university employees are allocated 12 paid holidays annually.

Langdon W. Patrick

Emil Jones, Jr., 1973–Present

Emil Jones, Jr., has been a member of the Illinois General Assembly since 1973. On December 2, 2004, Emil Jones, Jr. was the second African-American to be elected as President of the Illinois State Senate. Elected to the Illinois Senate in 1982, President Jones serves as a member of the Senate Executive Committee and Vice Chair of the General Assembly Retirement System's Board of Trustees. As a member of the Illinois House from 1973 to 1983, he served as an Assistant Democratic Leader and Chairman of the Insurance Committee.

A product of Chicago's Democratic machine, he first became interested in politics when he enmeshed himself in the presidential campaign of John F. Kennedy in 1960 and served as an aide to Alderman Wilson Frost, a longtime Democratic Party insider, then the 34th Ward Democratic committeeman and chairman of the City Council Finance Committee. Senator Jones was one of the 34th Ward's top precinct captains. Jones, one of eight children raised by a truck driver father and a homemaker mother, learned politics early on in

Emil Jones, Jr.

life. His father, Emil Jones, Sr., also worked as a bailiff to a well-known Cook County Circuit Court judge, Duke Slater, and as a Democratic precinct captain in three wards. As a result of his father's political apparatus, the 34th Ward Organization turned out the largest votes among the city's black ward organizations.

President Jones has been a strong supporter and passionate about education issues throughout his service in the Illinois General Assembly. One of his most memorable legislative accomplishments was the passage of the continuing appropriation or entitlement for education, similar to Social Security on the national level. This legislative act increased per pupil spending for school districts throughout the state. He has also sponsored and supported legislation that would dedicate 50 percent of all new revenue to education. He also engineered legislation that directed millions of state dollars for disadvantaged public school students to classroom needs rather than administrative allocations. Jones also passed legislation to double the personal exemption on the state income tax to benefit working families.

Other legislative highlights that he is credited for include the passage of legislation to secure an individual's right to choose a clinical social worker over a psychiatrist and to have a third party reimburse the expenses in cases involving the state. He championed a minimum wage increase and pay equity for women and backed more state contracts for minority firms and reforms of how the legal system deals with capital crimes. He also included a $20 million special appropriations for the Gwendolyn Brooks Preparatory Academy, which serves a minority population of approximately 85 percent in the FY 05 budget so that Brooks' facilities would be equal to Northside Preparetory High School, which serves primarily majority white students. He also supports expanding legalized gambling to promote economic development for disenfranchised minority communities. Jones also believes in easing the reliance on property taxes as a means of supporting local schools. He feels that the income tax should be replaced by the property tax so that the wealthy can bear the burden of funding the public school system. For example, currently wealthy school districts, such as Lake Forest, Illinois, spend approximately $20,173 on each child compared to less economically deprived school districts, like Summit Hill School District 161, spends approximately $4,829 per pupil. In Chicago, school funding for students ranges from $2,759 at Von Schiller on the North Side to $8,582 per student at Farren School on the Southside, according to an analysis by school reform journal Cataylst. As a result, children living in school districts that have high property values perform better on standardized tests and achieve better than students in low-income areas because their per pupil funding is much higher, as well as better trained and higher paid teachers More advanced technology and curriculum are the norm in these wealthy districts. Under the proposal that President Jones supports, this inequality would be eliminated. All public school children would receive an equal education. He also champions set-a-sides for minority contracting so that they can get their fair share of state funding projects, which includes money management for the state pension funds system. He also pushed for the passage of the Moratorium of the Death Penalty.

President Jones is also known for his support of building African-American institutions. He has provided state dollars for initiatives such as the following: a new library and Convocation Center for Chicago State University; $12 million for a new Kennedy-King College located in Englewood; $500,000 for a Diversity Institute at Northern Illinois University; funding to build the new Bronzeville Children Museum; funding for the new Beverly Arts Center; a $10 million special appropriation for the DuSable Musuem of African American History; $4 millions grant to the Muntu Dance Troupe; funding for a new baseball stadium for the Jackie Robinson Little League in the Beverly/Morgan Park community; grants for the construction of the AKA and Delta sororities on the southside of Chicago; $4 million for a children homes for HIV/AID victims in Englewood; and funding for the Southwest Side Women's Shelter. He is also a co-sponsor of SB 1, which provides funding for breast cancer research by providing a scratch-off on the Illinois Lottery.

Jones credits his ascension to leadership and his ability to get things done to his ability to put together coalitions, recognizing the needs of groups and their interests and not based on personal needs and desires. His style of leadership is based on the famous book, *Art of War*, by Sun Tzu. The theme of the book is that when one engages in a battle, one can be successful knowing more about the enemy than himself. "One has to know what they think and what impacts them and understand their interests," said President Jones in an interview. Jones added that, "he always remembers the advice that former Representative Ray Ewell gave him when he was elected to the Illinois House in 1973. Ewell advised me to get to know downstate legislators. Learn what their interests are and work with them to build a strong coalitions and you will succeed," said Jones.

Jones is credited for being the mentor for U.S. Senator Barack Obama.

Jones graduated from Chicago's Tilden Technical High School and Loop Junior College. He attended Roosevelt University. President Jones received an Honorary Doctor of Human Letters Degree from Chicago State University on June 1, 2001. Roosevelt University also bestowed the Honorary Doctorate to him in 2004.

He is also a graduate of Chicago State University.

James C. Taylor, 1969–1981; 1983–1985; 1981–1983

James C. Taylor was born February 8, 1930 in Crawfordsville, Arkansas. Prior to moving to Chicago, he lived in Memphis, Tennessee. He moved his family to Chicago, Illinois and attended Crane High School and later matriculated at the University of Illinois-Champaign and Monticello College. He served in the Korean War. After the war, he worked in the field of transportation. He was also a professional boxer. Taylor was elected to the House in 1968 and later to the Illinois Senate in 1981. He then returned to the House in 1983. As an elected official, he advocated for schools, police and local government legislation.

James C. Taylor

Richard A. Carter, 1971–1975

Richard A. Carter was born in Chicago, Illinois. He graduated from Crane High School and Morehouse College. He served in World War II, receiving five Battle Stars. After service to the U.S. Army, he worked in various positions with the City of Chicago. In 1971, he was elected to the Illinois House.

Jesse D. Madison, 1975–1979

Jesse D. Madison was born on January 1, 1939 in Memphis, Tennessee. In 1956, moved to Chicago, Illinois and attended Wilson Junior College and transferred to Roosevelt University where he earned his Bachelor's Degree in Business Administration. In 1974, he was elected to the Illinois House. While serving in the House, he was a voice for public aid recipients and he also fought for and passed the adult education legislation. After serving in the General Assembly, he went on to serve as Vice-President of Finance for the Chicago Urban League. Mayor Harold Washington later tapped Madison to serve as Commissioner of Consumer Services for the administration. He also served as Commissioner of the Chicago Park District. He retired as the President and CEO of the Abraham Lincoln Centre. Madison now serves as a member of the Illinois Prison Review Board.

Charles E. Gaines, 1975–1981

Charles E. Gaines, a Republican, was born on January 16, 1924 in Chicago, Illinois. He was the son of former Representative Harris B. Gaines. He attended Fisk University and the University of Illinois. He earned his law degree from John Marshall Law School and his graduate degree from Loyola University School of Social Work. Gaines worked in various social service positions and later was elected to the Illinois House in 1975. As a member, he pushed for legislation for senior citizens and other measures.

Charles E. Gaines

Taylor Pouncey, 1975–1983

Taylor Pouncey was born on January 9, 1923 in Carbondale, Illinois. He later moved to Chicago and graduated from Wendell Phillips High School. He served in the U.S. Marine Corps during World War II. After serving in the military, he worked in various government positions. In 1974, he won a seat to the Illinois House. As a veteran, he championed laws for assistance for Vietnam Veterans. He was active in the 16th Ward Democratic Organization.

Taylor Pouncey

Douglas Huff, Jr., 1975–1989

Douglas Huff, Jr., was born on January 8, 1931, in Chicago, Illinois. He was active in the Westside 21 Planning Commission. He attended Crane Junior College and Roosevelt University. Huff also served in the U.S. Army. He was

Douglas Huff, Jr.

elected to the Illinois House in 1974. He served on the Public Utilities, Personnel and Pensions, House, Appropriations, Election Laws and School District Reorganization committees. As a member of the School District Reorganization, he sponsored the school reform law (H.B. 4101), which proposed to: revise the Chicago public school structure by providing for a 15 member board; creation of the school management council, known today as the Local School Council; changing the way board members were appointed; how principals were selected; family choice in selecting where their children would attend school; giving the local school council the right to approve the school improvement plan; giving the right of the council to approve the school's budget; providing parents the right to take off time to pick up their children report cards; and providing maternity leave for teachers. He also sponsored public aid legislation, unemployment insurance and workmen's compensation legislation.

Jesse White, 1975–1992

Jesse White, served in the Illinois House of Representatives for sixteen years, representing the most culturally, economically, and racially diverse district in Illinois. His district made up the economically privileged Gold Coast and the economically impoverished Cabrini-Green public housing community. He became Cook County Recorder of Deeds in 1993 and was reelected in 1996. One of Mr. White's proudest accomplishments is when he founded the internationally known Jesse White Tumbling Team to serve as a positive alternative for children residing in Chicago's Cabrini-Green and Henry Horner public housing communities. Since its inception in 1959, more than 8,400 young men and women have performed with the team. White has spent more than

Jesse White

forty-four years working as a volunteer with the team to help kids stay away from drug, alcohol, gangs, and smoking, and to help set at-risk youth on the path to success. The program has received international praise. While a member of the Illinois legislature, White pushed through legislation that allows organizations that sponsored events that have an abundance amount of food leftover from an event can donate the food to shelters or other disadvantaged organizations without being concerned about liability, which was one of his major accomplishments while serving as a member of the Illinois House.

White served in the U.S. Army and the Illinois National Guard. He played professional baseball with the Chicago Cubs. He served as a teacher and administrator with the Chicago Public Schools for over thirty-three years. Mr. White earned his B.S. Degree from Alabama State College in 1957 and now resides on the near-north side of Chicago. In 1998, he became the first African American elected as Secretary of State in the Illinois.

Earlean Collins, 1976–1994

State Senator Earlean Collins, an independent and from the Westside of Chicago, was elected to the Illinois Senate in 1976. She was the first African-American female to serve in the Illinois Senate, the first female to serve as Assistant Majority Leader, and in 1994, the first African-American woman to wind the nomination for statewide office as the Democratic candidate for State Comptroller. Ms. Collins, along with former Senator Margaret Smith, was the first African-American to join their spouses in service to the State of Illinois. Her husband, Otis Collins, also served as an Independent in the General Assembly from 1965 to 1967. After twenty-two years of serving in the Illinois State Senate, she was elected as a member of the Cook County Board of Commission.

Earlean Collins

Senator Collins is best known for being the chief sponsor of the Earnfare Program, which is an innovative welfare reform program that assists welfare recipients entering the work force. She also sponsored legislation that established the Job Training Partnership Act, the Illinois Public Labor Relations Act, the Youth Education Incentive Employment Program, the Child Care Training Institute, and the Homeless Shelter Program. She championed legislation that assisted in the reduction of child abandonment and was the principle co-sponsor of the Women and Minority Business Assistance Program and the Illinois Housing Trust Program.

Collins served as an Assistant Majority Leader in the Illinois Senate and now serves as Commissioner for Cook County in Illinois.

Walter Shumpert, 1977–1979

Walter Shumpert, a native of Marion, Arkansas, was born on January 20, 1933. He attended Crane Junior College. He held various city and county positions. He was elected to the Illinois House in 1976 and resigned in 1979 to serve on the Chicago City Council.

Ethel Skyles Alexander, 1979–1987; Senate 1987–1993

Ethel Skyles Alexander was born on January 16, 1925 in Chicago, Illinois. She graduated from Englewood High School. She earned her Associate of Arts degree from Loop College, now Harold Washington College. Her father, Charles Skyles, also served in the Illinois House of Representatives. Ethel was the first woman to be appointed Assistant Chief Deputy Clerk of the

Ethel Skyles Alexander

Criminal Division of the Circuit Court. She was elected to the Illinois House in 1978. After the death of the late Senator Charles Chew, Jr., she was appointed to the Illinois Senate in 1986. While a member of the Illinois General Assembly, she championed legislation that prohibited state agencies from trading with South Africa apartheid government and sponsored laws that strengthen child pornography.

Larry Bullock, 1979–1987

Larry S. Bullock was born on April 14, 1946 in Winston-Salem, North Carolina. Bullock was a trailblazer in that he was the first African-American student who was admitted to Catawba Colleges in Salisbury, North Carolina where he earned a Bachelor's Degree in Political Science and moved to Chicago, Illinois and matriculated at Roosevelt University. He earned a Masters Degree in Public Administration. Upon graduation, he taught school in Evanston, Illinois. While a school teacher, he became active in Operation Push, where he was mentored by the Reverend Jesse Jackson, Sr. . He also became involved in local politics on the Southside of Chicago Second Ward. He ran against Alderman William Barnett; however; he was unsuccessful. In 1978, he successfully ran for state representative. While a member of the Illinois House, he sponsored legislation that expanded the McCormick Place. He also championed rights of nursing home residents, public aid recipients, workmen's compensation and small and minority businesses initiatives. Bullock was a very ambitious young man. In 1986, he ran for the seat of the First Congressional District that was held by Congressman Charles A. Hayes. He lost to the incumbent. Bullock's career took a downward turn. After an investigation of the misuse of public funds, he was tried and convicted and sentenced to four years in prison.

Larry Bullock

Carol Moseley-Braun, 1979–1988

Carol Moseley-Braun was born in Chicago on August 16, 1947. She graduated from the University of Illinois at Chicago and attended the University of Chicago Law School on a scholarship and received her J.D. Degree in 1972. She served five terms in the Illinois House of Representative. She was appointed as Assistant Majority Leader in the Illinois House of Representatives from 1978-1988. The late Mayor Harold Washington appointed her as his legislative floor leader. Braun was a co-sponsor of the School Reform Act. She championed legislation related to health care, asbestos removal from public schools, juvenile justice, homeless persons rights, minority and female set-asides on state funded projects, human rights, abolishing the Death Penalty Act and supported the Illinois Housing Development Act. In 1988-1992, she served as the first African-American Cook County Recorder of Deeds. In 1992, she was elected as the first women and first African-American woman in the U.S. Senate from Illinois.

In 1998, the former U.S. Senator Peter Fitzgerald, defeated Moseley-Braun as U.S. Senator. In 1999, she was appointed by President Clinton as the Ambassador to New Zealand, which was short-lived. President George Bush, Jr. named her replacement when he took office. In 2004, she entered the Democratic presidential nomination, which she lost to numerous Democratic opponents.

Carol Moseley-Braun

Quentin J. Goodwin, 1979–1981

Quentin J. Goodwin was born in New York. He graduated from Talladega College, in Alabama. He earned his law degree from Brooklyn Law School. He served in World War II. He later moved to Chicago, Illinois and became involved in the Second Ward Regular Democratic Organization. Goodwin was elected to the House of Representatives in 1979. He sponsored school integration and promotion legislation and other school related bills.

William C. Henry, 1979–1983

William "Bill" C. Henry was born in Greenwood, Mississippi on September 24, 1935. Like many southern African-Americans, he migrated to Chicago, Illinois with his family where he attended City Colleges of Chicago. He served in the U.S. Army. After his service to the military, he became involved in the 24th Democratic Organization. In 1964, he was appointed campaign manager for the late Congressman George Collins and continued in that role to his wife, Cardiss Collins, who ran for her late husband's congressional seat. In 1979, he was appointed to fill the unexpired term of State Representative Walter Shumpert, who resigned to assume the position of 24th Ward Committeeman. Henry was an advocate of economic development legislation and sponsored legislation to provide loans for slum areas.

William C. Henry

Clarence B. Williamson, 1980–1981

Clarence B. Williamson was born on June 1, 1930 in Chicago, Illinois. He earned his degree from Chicago State University. He was involved in the 6th Ward Democratic Organization. Williamson worked in the insurance industry and later worked in the field of corrections upon earning his graduate degree in Corrections. In 1980, he was appointed to fill the vacancy of Representative Eugene Barnes.

Clarence B. Williamson

Margaret Smith, 1981–2002

Senator Margaret Smith, a Democrat from Chicago, was the second female legislator to follow the footstep of her spouse, the late Senator Fred Smith, in the Illinois General Assembly. She served in the Illinois House of Representatives from 1981 to 1983 and the Illinois State Senate from 1983 to 2002. She was born in Chicago and attended Tennessee State University. She received an honorary Doctor of Humanities degree from the Chicago Baptist Institute.

While serving in the legislature, Senator Smith was known for her support of the Circuit Breaker assistance for senior citizens, sponsored and passed the Infant Mortality Reduction Act, and sponsored legislation that targeted preventing and helping teenaged mothers and their children. She was also responsible for the statue of Adelbert H. Roberts in the Illinois State Capital.

Margaret Smith

"I very proud of this statute because it honors the legacy of this great man," stated Smith in an interview shortly before her death. The Roberts memorial remains the only statue of an African-American person in any state capitol building in the nation and is the only public statue of an elected black official in Illinois. While serving in the Illinois legislature, she added a $500,000 grant for construction of a theater at the DuSable Museum of African-American History, increased state funding for elementary and secondary education in Chicago as well as the suburbs and downstate Illinois, and championed funding for road improvement projects in the 12the Legislative District.

Sylvester O. Rhem , 1981–1985

Sylvester O. Rhem was born in Chicago, Illinois on November 19, 1929. He graduated from Englewood High School. Rhem earned his Public Administration Degree from Roosevelt University. He held various positions with the Chicago Police Department and also worked for the U.S. Post Office as a mail carrier. He later worked with various social service organizations. Rhem was elected to the Illinois House of Representatives in 1990.

Sylvester O. Rhem

Arthur L. Turner, 1981–Present

Arthur L. Turner was born on December 2, 1950 in Chicago, Illinois. He earned his Bachelor's degree in Business Administration from Illinois State University and his Master of Science in Social Justice from Lewis University. After graduation, he held various positions with the Cook County State's Attorney Office. After Representative Jesse Madison resigned from his legislative seat, Turner was appointed to fill the vacancy. While in the Illinois

Arthur L. Turner

House, he sponsored the Affordable Housing Trust Funds Act, which he is known as "The Father of the Affordable Housing Funds Law."

Representative Turner currently serves as the Deputy Democratic Leader of the Illinois House of Representatives. While a member, he champions education, housing, energy and environment, consumer protection and insurance laws. He is the recipient of numerous public service and civic awards.

Jesse Jackson Sr., 1981–1983

Jesse Jackson Sr. was born in Memphis, Tennessee. He moved with his family to Chicago, Illinois while a teenager. He graduated from DuSable High School in 1942. Jackson was an entrepreneur. He owned a grocery store, sold auto parts and pursued a boxing career. He later worked for the Illinois Department of Transportation. Jackson was elected to the Illinois House in 1980.

Jesse Jackson Sr.

He sponsored legislation to provide for mandatory vaccine injury awards for children. He was also an advocate for small business development.

Monica Faith Steward, 1981-1983

Representative Monica Faith Steward was the youngest African-American female elected to the Illinois General Assembly in 1981. While a member of the Illinois House, she was instrumental in passing the Equal Rights Amendment to the Illinois Constitution. She graduated from Vassar College. She was born on September 3, 1952 in Chicago, Illinois.

Howard B. Brookins, 1983–1987

Howard B. Brookins was born in Chicago, Illinois on June 6, 1932. He graduated from DuSable High School and pursued his Associate of Arts Degree from Wilson Junior College. Brookins served in the Korean War. After the war, he worked for the U.S. Post Office and later worked for the Chicago Police Department. After serving as a police officer for numerous years, he matriculated at the Worsham College of Mortuary Science. In 1970, he bought a funeral home on the South Side of Chicago. In 1982, he was elected to the Illinois Senate. As a member of the Illinois Senate, he passed legislation allowing voters to register anywhere in the State of Illinois. Brookins was the primary sponsor of the judicial sub-circuit district law, which has increased the number of African American judges by 200 percent.

Howard B. Brookins

Ozie Hutchins, 1983–1985

Ozie Hutchins was elected to the Illinois House in 1982. While a member of the General Assembly, Hutchins advanced legislation related to consumer

Ozie Hutchins

fraud, low-income weatherization, minimum wage for the poor, public aid assistance for the economically disadvantaged and circuit-breaker legislation for the poor. He was forced to resign after he was convicted on extortion charges.

Sharon Markette, 1983–1985

Sharon Markette was born in Montgomery, Alabama on February 5, 1956. She earned her Bachelor's Degree in Criminal Justice from Chicago State University. After graduation, she worked for the State of Illinois Department of Employment Security. In 1983, she was appointed to replace Ozie Hutchins, who was convicted of extortion.

Sharon Markette

Robert LeFlore, Jr.

Robert LeFlore, Jr., 1983–1993

Robert LeFlore, Jr. was born in Carrolltown, Mississippi, on January 6, 1931. He served in the U.S. Army from 1951 to 1953. He was educated at Governors State University, in University Park, Illinois. He worked in the area of social services. In 1982, he was elected to the Illinois House of Representatives. In the Illinois House, he served as Chairman of the Illinois House Black Caucus (ILBC). He is credited with working effectively with all parties of the caucus to enhance the group's common purpose. As leader, he was instrumental in formalizing and bringing structure to the ILBC. During his tenure, the ILBC established formal by-laws, established its first bank account and created Joint Caucus Chairs in both the House and the Senate. LeFlore authored the School Reform Law. He also championed legislation related to public aid assistance, asbestos abatement, senior citizens, workmen's compensation, minority and female business economic development among other initiatives.

Nelson G.R. Rice, Sr., 1983–1993

Nelson G.R. Rice, Sr., was born in Chicago, Illinois on October 22, 1932. He earned his Master's Degree in Intercultural Studies from Governors State University. He pursued a career as a social worker. In 1982, he was elected to the Illinois House of Representatives, representing the Roseland community and other areas of the 34th Ward. Rice championed employment training, consumer training, public aid and funding for public schools.

Nelson G.R. Rice, Sr.

Mary E. Flowers, 1985–Present

Mary E. Flowers was born in Inverness, Mississippi, on July 31, 1951. Like most African-Americans who grew up in the south, she moved to Chicago, Illinois with her family. She graduated from Simeon High School on the Southside of Chicago. After graduation, she attended Kennedy-King College and the University of Illinois at Chicago. In the early 1980's, she volunteered in the campaign of the late Mayor Harold Washington. In 1984, she ran for the Illinois House of Representatives and was elected to serve as State Representative on the Southside of Chicago. While in the General Assembly, she has championed health care and children's rights legislation. She also fought for legislation to divest funds in South Africa. In 1999, Representative Flowers sponsored the Illinois Managed Care Act. She also was the chief sponsor of the Illinois Hospital Report Card Act, which requires hospital to make information available to the public about the quality of care that physicians provide. Flowers spearheaded the legislation to create a comprehensive physi-

Mary E. Flowers

cian profile database. Flowers is credited for taking the lead on renaming the Calumet Expressway after Bishop Louise Henry Ford.

William "Bill" Shaw, 1983–1993; 1993–2004

William "Bill" Shaw was born in Fulton, Arkansas on July 31, 1937. He moved to St. Louis, Missouri with his family. He later moved to Chicago and graduated from Crane High School. Shaw became active in 34th Ward Alderman Wilson Frost Ward Organization. In 1982, he was elected to the Illinois House of Representatives. In 1993, he went on to serve as State Senator. In 1997, he increased his power by being elected Mayor of Dolton, Illinois, while serving in the Illinois Senate. As a member of the Illinois Senate, he fought for legislation to increase the foundation level for public school children to a minimum of $4,225. In 2003, Reverend James Meeks, the flamboyant pastor of Salem Baptist Church, defeated Shaw when he ran as an independent in the South suburbs. This election was viewed as change in guard from the Regular Democratic Machine to more Independent and young individuals being elected to represent what had been traditionally been a Democratic strong whole. Meeks was supported by the young Congressman Jesse Jackson, Jr., while Shaw was supported by Senate President Emil Jones, Jr., who is part of the regular Democratic Organization.

Jerry Washington, 1985–1987

Jerry Washington, a Republican, was born in Merrigold, Mississippi, on December 23, 1940. He moved with his family to the Chicago area and attended

Jerry Washington

Bloom Township High School in Chicago Heights and later graduated from Dunbar Vocational High School in Chicago. After graduating from high school, he attended Wilson Junior College and Northwestern University. In 1984, he was elected as a Republican in the Illinois House of Representatives. While a member of the House, he collaborated with Democratic Senator Howard Brookins to expand the DuSable Museum of African American History. Washington also pushed for workmen's compensation, senior citizens, and funding for youth employment programs.

Paul Williams, 1986–1992

State Representative Paul L. Williams, an attorney and a Democrat, was elected in 1986, to represent the 24th District on the Southside of Chicago. He was tapped by the late Mayor Harold Washington and former Alderman Dorothy Tillman, of the Third Ward, to represent the areas, which comprised the Garfield Park/Washington Park, Grand Boulevard and Englewood communities. He, along with Representatives Anthony Young and Senators Howard Brookins and MiGuel DeValle, initiated the judicial sub-district legislation, which increased the number of African-American judges by 200 percent . Not only have African-Americans benefited from this historic legislation, Latinos, women, and gays have benefited substantially in counties throughout Illinois. According to an analysis in the October, 2004 *Illinois Issues,* this was the most profound legislation in the past three decades. This legislation brought about significant policy and institutional change that have empowered diverse communities politically and socially. In the October 1990 edition of the *Chicago Magazine,* he was named as "One of the Best Legislators." As a member, he is credited for single handedly saving funding for

Paul Williams

health clinics in the Chicago Public high schools. He also fought against the passage of the Chicago home equity legislation, which would infer the mire presence of African-American communities would devalue property values. The watered down version finally passed.

While serving as a member of the Illinois House, he served on the Judicial I and II Committees, Insurance, Consumer Protection, State Government Administration, and Housing. Because of his intellectual tenacity, he ascended to the leadership position of Democratic Floor Leader under the leadership of Speaker Michael J. Madigan. He also served as Secretary for the Illinois House Black Caucus.

He graduated from Chicago State University with a Degree in History Education. He holds a Master's Degree from the University of Illinois at Springfield and a J.D. from DePaul University School of Law.

In 1992, he established his own independent lobbying and law firm. His principle areas of concentration are legislative affairs and real estate transactions.

Anthony Young, 1985–1992

Representative Anthony Young, a Democrat, was born in Chicago. He was elected to the Illinois House from the Westside of Chicago. He earned his undergraduate degree in Business Administration from Golden State University. He earned his law degree from DePaul University. He, along with Representative Paul Williams and Senators Howard Brookins and Miguelle DeValle, pushed through the judicial sub-district legislation. While serving in the House, he was appointed Deputy Majority Leader by Speaker Madigan.

Anthony Young

Louvana S. Jones, 1986–2006

Lovana "Lou" Jones was elected to the Illinois House of Representatives in 1986 from the 26th District, which is located on the south side of Chicago. She served as Assistant Majority Leader in the House. She was a strong advocate of children and women's issues and a vocal leader for reforming the state correctional system. Jones also sponsored legislation to divest $2 billion in state funds from Sudan.

She was active in both political and civic affairs. She joined Operation Breadbasket, the predecessor to Operation Push, during its inception in 1968. Representative Jones received numerous awards from various community organizations during her career in the Illinois legislature.

She was born in Mansfield, Ohio. Her family moved to Illinois in 1959. She earned her Bachelor's of Arts Degree in Business Administration from Ohio State University.

Louvana S. Jones

Monique D. Davis, 1987–Present

Monique D. Davis was born in Chicago, Illinois on August 19, 1936. She earned her Bachelor's Degree in Elementary Education and a Master's Degree in Guidance and Counseling from Chicago State University. Davis got involved in the campaign of former Congressman Gus Savage, the late Mayor Harold Washington and former Representative Monique Faith Steward. She successfully ran and was elected to the Illinois House of Representatives in 1986.

"One of the most influential events in my career was when I visited with Nelson Mandela on a trip to South Africa with Governor George Ryan and other elected officials. I was selected to be a part of the delegation because of the work that my church, Trinity United Church of Christ, had done to abolish apartheid in South Africa," said Davis.

Monique D. Davis

As a member of the House of Representatives, she has brought home resources to her district such as funding to add an addition to the Vivian Harsh Collection Building to the Carter G. Woodson Library. She has worked to bring funding to address the HIV health crises in the African-American community, increase funding of over $400 million for the elementary secondary schools in Illinois, saved City Colleges with an addition of over $16 million for 2004 and 2005, brought funding for Brainerd and Wrightwood Libraries, and fought for funding for the Financial Outreach Center and other infrastructure enhancements at Chicago State University.

Davis is also credited for passing laws that prevents the selling of drug paraphernalia, video taped confessions for capital cases, video taped interrogations, racial profiling study, and changed the required testing before students teach in Illinois in order to allow students opportunities in the field of teaching. As an educator, Davis is persistent in fighting to equalize state funding for all public school children in Illinois.

Representative Davis mentors young people by providing them with volunteer opportunities in her legislative office.

Charles G. Morrow, 1987–2005

Charles G. Morrow was born in Chicago on July 21, 1956. He graduated from DeLaSalle High School. Morrow attended the Illinois Institute of Technology. In 1986, he was elected to the Illinois House of Representatives. While a member of the Illinois House, he fought diligently to increase the share of state funding for minority contractors. As Chairman of the Transportation Committee, he fought diligently to make certain that the Dan Ryan Expressway receive state funding to repave the Dan Ryan, which serves mainly the African-American community. Other expressways in the City of Chicago that serve primarily White communities had been included in the transportation budget to get

Charles G. Morrow

their share of state dollars for reconstruction. Before Morrow lost his election to the Illinois House, he also spearheaded the fight to increase the number of African-Americans contractors on the Dan Ryan Expressway construction site. According to a transportation study, African-Americans only make up 4 percent of 10 percent of contracts on the Dan Ryan Expressway. Morrow was also concerned about the welfare of children. He fought for a $5 million childcare center to be constructed at Chicago State University. This center provides a safe and educational focused learning environment for children of Chicago State University's students and the surrounding community.

Shirley M. Jones, 1987–2002

Shirley M. Jones was born in Chicago, Illinois on November 9, 1939. She attended George Williams College. Jones was elected to the Illinois House of

Shirley M. Jones

Representatives on 1986. She championed legislation for seniors, public aid, criminal justice and consumer rights. She served as chair of the Public Utilities Committee that wrote the utility deregulation measure that revamped the system for Illinois.

Donne E. Trotter, 1988–Present

Senator Donne E. Trotter was elected to the Illinois House of Representatives in 1988. He was elected to the Illinois Senate in 1992. He serves as the Chairman of the powerful Appropriations I Committee and is the chief budget negotiator for the Democrats. As Chair of Appropriations I, he oversees all budget initiatives for the state's $53 million budget. He ensures that the disadvantaged are partners in the wealth of the state for enforcing parity in education and health care and creating economic development and redevelopment of depressed communities. He also champions the equitable distribution of contracts and jobs to all geographic and ethnic communities. Senator Trotter also spearheaded and passed legislation closing the worst landfills and incinerators on the southeast side of Chicago. Senator Trotter ushered in Illinois' first comprehensive law banning assault weapons. He was also instrumental in creating and expanding the KidCare Family Care and Senior Care initiatives. By increasing the eligibility threshold, over 270,000 children and their parents benefit from this initiative. He is also a strong advocate for drug affordability. Senator Trotter sponsored the "Safe Haven" Act. This legislation allows parents of newborns to surrender their infants at hospitals, firehouses and other "safe havens" without fear of criminal charges. This act saves many newborn lives. The law is aimed at confused and panicked parents who might otherwise abandon their child in the trash or on the street. The

Donne E. Trotter

idea of providing a safe and legal way for parents to abandon babies has swept the nation. Fourty-seven states have enacted safe-haven laws since 1999.

Nationally, Senator Trotter is actively involved with the National Conference of State Legislators and the National Black Caucus of State Legislators. Senator Trotter was born in Cairo, Illinois. He attended the Chicago Public Schools. He graduated from Chicago State University with a B.A. degree in Political Science/History and is a graduate of Loyola University School of Law with a Master's Degree in Health/Policy and Law.

Alice Palmer, 1991–1996

Alice Palmer was born in Indianapolis, Indiana on June 20, 1939. She earned her Bachelor's Degree from Indiana University in 1965. She taught school for a brief period of time in the Indiana school system. Palmer later moved to Chicago and worked at Malcom X Junior College. She went on to earn her Master's Degree from Roosevelt University and later her Ph.D. from Northwestern University. After graduation, she held various executive level positions. Palmer got involved in politics when she was active in the school reform movement. Her goal was to equalize funding for all public school children with respect to the State of Illinois Constitution. She worked closely with community groups such as the Chicago Urban League and other activists and bi-partisan groups toward this goal. As part of this effort, she founded the City Schools partnership between schools and corporations. In 1991, Palmer was appointed to replace the late Senator Richard Newhouse because of her involvement with the independent movement for over twenty years. As a member of the Illinois Senate, she was a strong advocate for education, envi-

Alice Palmer

ronmental economic development legislation, health care and a living wage for home health care workers, and the advancement for women health initiatives. Palmer also secured funding for women transitioning off welfare so that they could start their own businesses. Palmer now works at the University of Illinois at Chicago in the College of Urban Planning and Public Affairs.

Calvin L. Giles, 1993–2007

Calvin L. Giles was born in Chicago, Illinois on July 10, 1963. Giles earned his Bachelor's Degree from Northeastern Illinois University. At an early age, he became interested in politics by working in the office of his uncle, former alderman Percy Giles, Alderman of the 37th Ward and for the late mayor Harold Washington. In 1993, Giles was appointed to fill the vacancy of Robert LeFlore after he passed. While a member of the Illinois House, Giles co-sponsored legislation appropriating $10 million toward the construction of a new library in Oak Park, Illinois. Giles served as House Caucus Chair of the Illinois Legislative Black Caucus.

Calvin L. Giles

Rickey Hendon, 1993–Present

Rickey Hendon, a Democrat, was born in Cleveland, Ohio on December 8, 1953. His family moved to Chicago, Illinois. When he entered high school, his family moved to Detroit, Michigan. After graduation, he earned an FCC license which further his career in radio broadcasting. Later, Hendon moved back to Chicago and got involved in local politics, which lead to his appointment as Committeeman of the 27th Ward by the late Mayor Harold Washington. In 1987, Hendon was elected to the City Council to represent the 27th

Rickey Hendon

Ward. He was later elected to the Illinois State Senate. In 1997, he was elected Senate Chairperson of the Illinois Legislative Black Caucus. In 2002, Senate President Emil Jones appointed him as Senate Majority Leader. "I am proud of my efforts to bring more economic development resources to the Westside of Chicago than any legislators has ever done. The Westside now receives its fair share of state resources in many ways. As a result, the Westside is thriving as far as the value of housing and the desire of citizens to live on the Westside," said Hendon. Hendon was also the original sponsor of the Racial Profiling Legislation and the Death Penalty Law. Hendon is also known for bringing the movie business to the City of Chicago through his support of the tax credit for the industry. He is also responsible for getting rid of prostitution up and down Madison Street on the Westside, which has also helped to attract economic development to the Westside of Chicago. As a member of the Illinois Senate, Hendon views his main role as the backbone and supporter of Senate President Emil Jones, Jr. and to serve as his number one supporter on the Illinois Senate Floor and in the Democratic Caucus. "I got his back," said Hendon.

Senator Hendon is a mentor of many up and coming leaders on the West Side such as Patricia Horton, who heads the Successful Independent Network. This organization helps women, female and community based businesses write grants. Also, he mentors Roger Chandler, the president of the Democratic Westside Organization. As an avid softball player, he mentors many young men, not only in helping to enhance their athletic skills, but also to help them navigate college, life and to help them identify employment opportunities.

Constance "Connie" A. Howard, 1995–Present

Representative Connie Howard was born on December 14, 1942, in Chicago, Illinois and raised in Woodlawn. She graduated from Hyde Park High School.

Constance "Connie" A. Howard

Representative Howard graduated from Chicago Teacher's College with a B.A. in liberal arts and earned a Master's Degree from Chicago State University in Correction and Criminal Justice.

Representative Howard was elected to the Illinois House of Representatives in 1995 to represent the 34th District on the Southside of Chicago, which includes a major portion of the southeast side of Chicago as well as the southern suburbs. While in the Illinois House of Representatives, she has been a passionate voice to fund the fight against AIDS in the African-American community, supported legislation to advance the field of computer technology and worked on many criminal justice issues. She passed a law in the Illinois legislature to make expungement possible in the state of Illinois. Expungement is the erasing of a conviction of an ex-offender who has committed a less severe offense or a misdemeanor, as well as those persons who were falsely accused, convicted, and subsequently found to be innocent by DNA or other evidence and/or a court trail. She is also passionate about making certain that all citizens, especially African-Americans, have access to computers and information technology. As a result of her initiative and other leaders, African American usage of high-speed internet has soared from 14 percent in 2005 to 40 percent in 2007, according to a study released by the Pew Foundation. During the spring 2005 session of the Illinois General Assembly, Howard introduced legislation allowing prostitutes to sue pimps. The intent of the legislation is to empower men, women and children trapped in desperate situations. Under the measure, prostitutes would have to prove in court that the pimp profited from the sex trade, recruited prostitutes or trafficked and maintained them. The pimp could be held accountable for his victim's financial losses, personal injuries, diseases and mental and emotional anguish.

Representative Howard has a solid history as a political strategist, campaign worker and community leader. She served as a District Coordinator in the 1983 and 1987 campaigns of Mayor Harold Washington. In 1992, she co-ordinated the South Side Chicago office of Moseley-Braun for U.S. Senate and Clinton for President campaign. The late Senator Cecil Partee and Mayor Harold Washington appointed her to the position of Democratic State Committeeman as the female representative from the First Congressional District in 1984. She was also elected as an alternate delegate to the Democratic National Convention in 1984 and 1988, and served as a member of the Rules Committee for the 1996 National Convention in Chicago.

Deborah L. Graham, 2003–Present

Deborah L. Graham, Democrat and Chicago native from the west side, was elected to the Illinois House in 1993. She holds a Bachelor's Degree in Business Administration from Robert Morris College. Graham become active in the community while working along side of her grandmother early in life in church as well as helping to feed the homeless and working as an advocate for senior citizens.

As a legislator, she has worked with senior groups to pass long-term care reforms and measures to protect seniors from exploitation. She also has been instrumental in closing loopholes related to ex-offenders failing to register as sex offenders and has championed legislation that requires stricter gun control laws. Graham is a strong advocate of education accountability of education agencies relative to public school children. She is also an advocate of child safety transportation laws.

Graham has worked in various positions in the City of Chicago government.

Deborah L. Graham

Coy Pugh, 1993–2001

Coy Pugh was born in Chicago, Illinois on February 27, 1952. He graduated from St. Mel Catholic High School on the Westside of Chicago. He earned an undergraduate degree from Northeastern University Inner City Studies. He also earned his Master's of Divinity Degree from The McCormick Theological Seminary. As a young adult, he served time in the Illinois correctional system. Along the way, he matured and became interested in politics. He was taken under the wings of former State Representative Anthony Young, now judge, as a mentor. After Young was elected to the judiciary, Pugh ran for his mentor's legislative seat and was successful in 1992. While a member of the Illinois House, he championed the abolition of the Death Penalty Act. He is now an independent lobbyist and an entrepreneur.

Coy Pugh

Todd H. Stroger, 1993–2001

Todd H. Stroger was born in Chicago, Illinois on January 14, 1963. Stroger attended St. Ignatius College Preparatory. He earned his degree from Xavier University in New Orleans. He is an investment banker. Stroger was elected to the Illinois House in 1992 until he was elected Alderman of the 8th Ward after the death of Lorraine Dixon. While a member of the Illinois House, he sponsored legislation that would allow teaching assistants and graduate assistants to become unionized. He is the son of former Cook County President John Stroger. Todd now serves as President of the Cook County Board, succeeding his father in this powerful position.

Howard A. Kenner, 1995-2003

Howard Kenner was born in Chicago, Illinois on December 26, 1957. He earned his accounting degree from the University of Illinois. Kenner was

Todd H. Stroger

elected to the Illinois House of Representatives in 1994. He is the son of for-
mer Third Ward Alderman Tyrone Kenner. He is the founder of the Third
Ward Young Democratic Organization and served as a precinct captain of the
Third Ward.

Barack Obama, 1997–2005

Barack Obama was first elected to the Illinois Senate in 1997. Obama, a Harvard educated lawyer, worked as a community organizer in the Altgeld Gar-
dens Housing projects organizing against environmental racism and also was
later asked to run for the Senate seat being vacated by Senator Alice Palmer.
Once elected, he became known for his ability to forge compromises across
party lines.

Barack Obama

While serving in the State Senate, he gained notice for his sponsorship and passage of the Illinois Ethics Reform Act. This was a big bipartisan effort to rein in Illinois wide open campaign contributions. This law bans nearly all gifts by lobbyists and bars the personal sue of campaign money. Such high profile figures as former U.S Senator Paul Simon co-authored the study that lead to the Ethics Reform Act. Obama also championed broadening the Open Meetings Act, which mandates that, all meeting involving governmental entities must be open to the general public.

Barack also sponsored legislation and policies that specifically benefited the minority communities that he represented. Obama sponsored and passed the "driving while black or DWB" legislation while in the Illinois state Senate. The Act known as the 2003 Traffic Stop Statistics Act, requires police to note race, time location and several other details during every traffic stop. By requiring the collection of such data, the law hoped to discourage the use of race as a pretense for racial motivated stops and to provide data and proof of the alleged practice. In 2005, the Illinois Department of Transportation used this data to show that African American motorists were stopped 27 percent higher than their population. Obama also pushed to get state run pension funds to open opportunities for minority money managers and lead Democratic negotiators on a landmark welfare to work package that Republicans were pushing. Obama was a strong advocate for equitable funding for all public schools, juvenile justice reform and an expansion of health care coverage. He also pushed for the creation of an office to provide assistance to immigrants.

In 1983, Obama earned his Bachelor's Degree from Columbia University in New York and graduated from Harvard Law School in 1991. He was the first African American president of the prestigious Harvard Law Review. He was elected to the US Senate as the first African American male U.S. Senator from Illinois in 2005. He embarked on a Presidential campaigned that has out fund raised any previous candidate to date in terms of number of contributors.

Kwame Raoul, 2004–Present

Kwame Raoul of Chicago was appointed to represent the 13th Legislative District, succeeding Barack Obama. Senator Raoul earned his Bachelor's Degree in Political Science from DePaul University and a Juris Doctorate from Chicago-Kent College of Law. He is a former Cook County prosecutor and now serves as senior attorney for the City Colleges of Chicago. The Senator is also the founder and director of the Janin and Marie Raoul Foundation in memory of his late father and mother, who now resides in Florida. The foundation promotes healthcare as a human right.

Kwame Raoul

As a member of the Illinois Senate, he champions African-American and minority equitable participation in Illinois pension investment initiatives, as well as a strong advocate of school funding equity for all public school children and access to health care for the working poor. Senator Raoul also has sponsored gun-control legislation and domestic violence laws.

Wanda Sharp, 1999–2000

Wanda Sharp was born in Chicago, Illinois on July 23, 1950. She served as a committeewoman for Proviso Township and the Village of Maywood. In 1999, she was appointed to replace former Representative Eugene Moore, who was elected as Cook County Recorder of Deeds. While a member of the Illinois House, Sharp sponsored legislation encouraging voter registration among former inmates.

Wanda Sharp

Marlow H. Colvin, 2001–Present

Marlow H. Colvin was born Chicago, Illinois in March 1964. He earned his Bachelor's Degree in Political Science from Chicago State University. During his undergraduate work at Chicago State, Colvin received numerous awards including the Al Raby and Nancy Jefferson Memorial Awards from the History and Political Science Department. He was also inducted in the National Political Science Honor Society and was awarded a fellowship to the Ralph J. Bunche Summer Institute at the University of Virginia. Colvin replaced former Representative Todd Stroger in the Illinois House when Stroger was elected to the City Council, representing the Eight Ward. While a member of the House, Colvin has championed equal opportunity for minority contractors on state projects.

He serves as Chairman of the Illinois House Legislative Black Caucus.

Marlow H. Colvin

Annazette Collins, 2001–Present

Annazette Collins was born in Chicago, Illinois on April 28, 1962. She earned a Bachelor's Degree in Sociology from Northern Illinois University and a Master's Degree in Criminal Justice from Chicago State University. Collins was elected to the Illinois legislature in 2000, representing the Westside of Chicago. Collins has sponsored legislation focusing on juvenile justice. Representative Collins is the sponsor of legislation that raises the age of adulthood from 17 to 18 years old. This legislation prevents juveniles from having an adult criminal record and they would no longer suffer the lifetime barriers to employment and educational opportunities that come with an adult felony conviction. "In Illinois, seventeen years olds are unable to vote, serve in the armed forces, legally sign a contract, marry or buy cigarettes. However, they can spend the rest of their lives in an adult prison for committing a crime.

Annazette Collins

"This is not fair," added Collins. As part of this legislative effort, Collins also sponsored legislation creating the Department of Juvenile Justice.

Representative Collins is also proud of the law that expands the individual who are eligible to take legal custody of children. "Under the old law, only grandparents, uncle, and aunts could take legal custody. Now, second cousins, godparents and others closed to the young person can assume custody. I am very proud of this legislation that I sponsored, " said Collins.

Former Alderman Jesse Butler and Alderman Ed Smith, who encouraged her to run for the General Assembly seat, are her mentors.

As a member of the General Assembly, Collins said that some of the challenges she faces is being a female. "It is extremely hard to get her male colleagues to listen to women. Springfield is a chauvinistic environment that does not always welcome female voices," said Collins.

Mattie Hunter, 2002–Present

Senator Mattie Hunter was born in Chicago, Illinois. She earned her Bachelor of Arts from Monmouth College in Monmouth, Illinois and her Masters of Arts in Sociology from Jackson State University.

Senator Hunter is the recipient of numerous community and humanitarian awards. As a member of the Illinois Senate, she has passed numerous pieces of legislation such as Juneteenth National Day, a bill that bans the sale, distribution and manufacturing of mercury fever thermometers and other health related bills. She also sponsored legislation requiring a check-off provision of The Illinois Lottery for breast cancer research.

Mattie Hunter

Jacqueline Y. Collins, 2003–Present

Jacqueline "Jacquie" Collins was born in McComb, Mississippi. She studied journalism at Northwestern University and earned her Master's Degree from the John F. Kennedy School of Government at Harvard University. She also earned her M.A. in Human Services Administration from Spertus College and a M.A. in Theological Studies from Harvard Divinity School.

She had an illustrious career in broadcasting before entering politics. She is a former Emmy Award nominated news editor at CBS-TV in Chicago, Illinois.

Collins served as a fellow for U.S. Senator Hillary Rodham Clinton. She was elected to the Illinois Senate in 2002. While a member of the Senate, she champions the disinvestments of state funds in Sudan, Africa.

Jacqueline Y. Collins

Kenneth "Ken" Dunkin

Kenneth "Ken" Dunkin, 2003–Present

Ken Dunkin is a product of the Chicago Public School system. He earned his Associate of Arts Degree from Harold Washington College and his Bachelor's of Arts Degree from Morehouse College in Atlanta, Georgia. After graduating from Morehouse, he earned his Master's of Arts Degree in Social Service Administration from the University of Chicago.

Before representing the 5th District State Representative seat, he was director of the Robert Taylor Homes Boys and Girls Club. During his political career, Secretary of State Jesse White has served as his mentor. He also served as an intern for the late U.S. Senator Paul Simon. Since that time, he has worked in various administrative capacities and has served on numerous boards.

As a member of the Illinois House of Representatives, he sponsored legislation that extends tax credits to film producers to encourage them to bring more film industry to Illinois. He has also championed reducing domestic violence, sustaining and creating new businesses, preventing identity theft, reducing prescription drug prices for the elderly, improving academic achievement of students and providing affordable childcare and health care for the disadvantaged.

Patricia Bailey, 2003–2005

Representative Patricia Bailey was born in Chicago. She earned her Bachelor's Degree in Social Work from Chicago State University. Bailey was convicted of two felonies in November 2005, perjury and forgery and had to resign from the Illinois House of Representatives.

Patricia Bailey

Esther Golar, 2005–Present

Esther Golar was appointed to the Illinois House of Representatives to replace Patricia Bailey. Rep. Golar works with the Chicago Alternative Policing Strategy Program and has been a community activist for over 20 years. She attended Malcolm X College.

Chapter Three

Legislators Elected Outside of Cook County—1966 to Present

Kenneth Hall, 1966–1995

In 1966, Kenneth Hall, from East St. Louis, Illinois was elected to the House of Representatives. In 1972, he was elected to the Senate. From 1975 to 1985, he became the Senate's first African-American Assistant Majority Leader. He then was selected by the leadership of the Senate to serve as Chairman of the powerful Appropriations II Committee.

Before being elected to the Illinois legislature, he was appointed to the State Rent Control Board by Governor Adlai Stevenson from 1949-50 and served as Commissioner of the St. Clair County's Housing Authority, of which he was later appointed Chair. He was a former member of the St. Clair County Welfare Service Committee, Commissioner of the East St. Louis Park District. Hall served as a Democratic Precinct Committeeman for 28 years, and Chairman of East St. Louis City Democratic Central Committee.

Kenneth Hall

He graduated from Lincoln High School and was educated at Parks College in Cahokia, Illinois.

Wyvetter Younge, 1975–Present

Representative Wyvetter Younge, a Democrat, who represents East St. Louis, Illinois, earned her Bachelor's Degree from Hampton Institute in 1951 and her J.D. Degree from St. Louis University School of Law in 1955 and her LLM Degree in 1972 from Washington University School of Law. She is a former Assistant Circuit Attorney She has held various administrative and judicial positions during her career. She received "The Best Legislator Award"from the UAW in 1993. She is a staunch fighter for initiatives that help to sustain the economic viability of the deprived city of East St. Louis. She fights vigorously for economic development, affordable housing, employment and other measures that benefit her constituents.

Wyvetter Younge

Eugene "Gene" Moore, 1993–1999

Eugene "Gene" Moore was born in Baltzer, Mississippi, on July 19, 1942. He was educated at Otero College in Colorado. He is an insurance executive. Moore was elected to the Illinois House of Representatives in 1992. While a member of the Illinois House of Representatives, he fought for legislation related to education, criminal justice, senior citizens, public aid and child welfare, human rights, economic development opportunities for disadvantaged minorities and numerous other measures. He now serves as Cook County Recorder of Deeds.

Harold Murphy, 1993–2003

Harold Murphy was born in Birmingham, Alabama on April 1, 1938. He earned his teaching degree from Northeastern Illinois University. He was elected to the Illinois House in 1992.

James F. Clayborne, Jr., 1995–Present

Senator James F. Clayborne, Jr. was born in St. Louis, Missouri on December 29, 1963. He was sworn into office on April 17, 1995 to serve the remainder of the term of the late Senator Kenneth Hall. He earned his Bachelor's Degree from Tennessee State University in 1985 and his J.D. in 1988 from the University of Miami School of Law. He served as a law clerk for the United States District Court for the Southern District of Florida and as a clinical intern with then Dade County State's Attorney Janet Reno.

Senator Clayborne serves as Majority Caucus Whip for the 94th General Assembly. As a member of the Illinois Senate, he is a strong advocate for economic development, education and other infrastructure improvements. Throughout his career, he has been the recipient of numerous awards.

Clayborne is a partner in the firm of Hinshaw and Culbertson of Belleville and serves as Corporate Counsel for the City of East St. Louis. He is a member of the Wesley Bethel Methodist Church in East St. Louis and serves on various boards.

James F. Clayborne, Jr.

Kimberly A. Lightford, 1998–Present

Senator Kimberly A. Lightford, of Maywood, Illinois. She was born on May 10, 1968, in Chicago. She is the youngest African-American female to be

Kimberly A. Lightford

elected to the Illinois State Senate. Lighftord has served as chair of the Illinois Senate Black Caucus. As chair, her goal was to combine the resources of its members to strengthen communities throughout Illinois. While serving in the Illinois Senate, she is responsible for passing the Truth In-Sentencing Act; The Payday Loan Reform Act, which mandates caps on loans by this industry; legislation to increase the minimum wage from $5.15 to $6.50 an hour; legislation to help low-income children receive a hot breakfast while at school; a bill that gives scholarship incentives to teachers who teach in underserved areas; legislation to allow working mothers to have a private place at work to express milk for their babies; and initiatives to provide educational awareness and testing for HIV and AIDS and to increase prostate, cervical and breast cancer awareness. In addition, she is a staunch supporter of quality education for all children. Lightford is also credited for legislation requiring criminal background checks of Local School Council members.

Senator Lightford earned her Bachelor of Arts Degree from Western Illinois University in Communications and Human Relations and a Master's of Public Administration from the University of Illinois at Springfield. Prior to being elected to the Illinois Senate, she served as an intern for the Illinois House of Representatives, where she gained insights into the legislative process. This opportunity inspired her to seek elected office as a Trustee for the Village of Maywood from 1997 – 2003. As a young African-American female legislator and single parent, Senator Lightford has received numerous awards, honoring the many accomplishments that she has achieved. She serves on numerous boards.

Willis Harris, 1999-2001

Willis Harris was born in Mound Bayou, Mississippi on March 27, 1946. He completed his undergraduate degree at Mississippi Valley State University in Itta Bena, Mississippi. Harris was elected to the Illinois House in 1998, representing the area which incorporates Dolton, Illinois. He founded the Dolton Homeowners Association.

David E. Miller, 2001–Present

David E. Miller was born in Cleveland, Ohio on September 23, 1962. He earned his Bachelor's Degree in Biomedical Engineering from Boston University and earned a doctoral of dental surgery from the University of Illinois at Urbana-Champaign.

As a member of the Illinois House of Representatives, he has proposed programs and legislation to improve health care, equity in education funding for all public school children, economic viability, notably funding for a new airport in Peotone, Illinois that will serve primarily south suburban communities and consumer protection for his constituents. While a member of the Illinois House, he sponsored the Pay Day Loan Reform Act. He has received various awards and recognition.

David E. Miller

Karen Yarbrough, 2001–Present

Karen Yarbrough was born in Washington, D.C. on August 22, 1950. She earned her Bachelor's Degree in Business Administration from Chicago State University and a Master's Degree from Northeastern Illinois University Inner City Studies. She founded the Hathaway Insurance Agency. Karen served as President of the Maywood Chamber of Commerce for eight years, where she advocated for growth and stability in the community. Under her leadership, the Chamber established a program for honor roll students and initiated a business/education collaborative scholarship program for Proviso East students, which has awarded over $50,000 to deserving students.

Karen Yarbrough

Yarbrough was elected to the Illinois House in 2000, representing suburban communities of Maywood, Bellwood, Broadview, Forest Park, Hillside and parts of Oak Park, River Forest, Melrose Park, Westchester and the Austin community of Chicago. In 2006, Karen was elected as Proviso Township Democratic Committeeman. She is the first African-American and female to be elected to this position. Her goal is to heal divisions among Democrats in the highly Democratic Proviso Township area. Karen is the recipient of numerous awards.

As a member of the House, she champions education, health care and economic development initiatives and she is a strong advocate of government accountability and accessibility to the electorate.

Eddie Washington, 2002–Present

Eddie Washington was elected to the Illinois House of Representatives in 2002. He holds the distinction of being elected as the first African-American representative to serve from Lake County, Illinois in the state legislature. He is the radio talk show host of The Eddie Washington Journal.

Representative Washington was born in East St. Louis, Illinois and has lived in Waukegan for approximately 20 years. As a resident of Waukegan, he has been active in efforts to improve the community. He is the founder of People Organized Working for Equal Rights (POWER), which is a community activist group. He has worked as the former director of the Lake County Urban League and director for the Waukegan Township Staben Center. He is also actively involved with the Lake County NAACP and the John Howard Association.

In the Illinois House of Representatives, he supports fair lending practices, discount prescription drugs and consumer fraud protection for senior citizens,

Eddie Washington

economic development measures, equity in funding for all public school children, and fair criminal justice legislation.

Representative Washington other legislative accomplishments include: "The Little David" policy, which penalizes institutions for relining policies; insures domestic violence victims who are legal immigrants receiving social service resources that aid women and children; requires the Illinois Department of Public Health to develop rules for the training of certified medical technicians in nursing homes; and insures that railroad workers who are injured receive proper medical attention without interference. Representative Washington was named "The Most Influential African-American of Lake County."

Chuck Jefferson, 2001–Present

Chuck Jefferson is the first African-American elected as representative in Rockford, Illinois. African-American comprise only 15 percent of the 150,000 person population. Representative Jefferson commands the respect of the mainstream citizenry of Rockford, Illinois.

In the early 1980s, Jefferson became involved in grass root politics as a precinct caption. He served as campaign manager to the first African-American Mayor Charles Box of Rockford for twelve years. Throughout much of the 1990s, he served as Executive Vice-Chairman of the Winnebago County Democratic Central Committee. In 1990, Jefferson was elected the 6th District of the Winnebago County Board, where he has served as Chairman of the Public Works Committee.

Representative Jefferson's top concerns in the legislature are education, senior citizen issues, criminal justice and economic development. He is a member of the Winnebago County Board. Jefferson sponsored the judicial

Chuck Jefferson

sub-circuits legislation. Small judicial sub-circuits are created in Lake, McHenry, Will, Kane, Winnebago and Boone counties, with DeKalb and Kendall counties a possibilities, too. Currently, there are 150 judges who serve in Winnebago, County and none are African-American. "My goal is to increase the number of African-American judges elected in Winnebago County. Cook County is the only county that has sub-circuits," stated Representative Jefferson. This legislation was also sponsored by former Representatives Paul Williams, Anthony Young, and MiGuel DeValle.

Jefferson is one of eleven children and spent his early childhood years in Texas where he completed high school and took coursework at Paul Quinn College. In 1966, Jefferson joined the U.S. Army and rose to the rank of Sergeant. He served six years in Virginia, Japan, and Germany.

Robin L. Kelly, 2002–2006

Robin L. Kelly was born in New York City and moved to Illinois to attend college. She received her B.A. and Master's Degrees from Bradley University in Peoria, Illinois. Kelly earned her Ph.D. from Northern Illinois University.

As a member of the Illinois House, she champions economic development legislation, education funding for public schools and supports measures to address mass transit issues affecting the south suburbs. Kelly is proud of legislation that she sponsored to alleviate traffic accidents involving emergency vehicles. While serving in the legislature, she received numerous awards from various community organizations.

Robin L. Kelly

William "Will" Davis, 2003–Present

William "Bill" Davis was born in Harvey, Illinois on July 2, 1968. Davis earned his Bachelor's Degree from Southern Illinois University and is currently pursuing his Master's Degree from Governor's State University. While a member of the House, Davis' top priorities are equalization of education funding for students in grades K-12, financial aid for needy students, affordable prescription drugs for all senior citizens, economic development and revitalization of the south suburbs and other legislative initiatives that empower the community. He is a staunch supporter of the Abraham Lincoln National Airport in Peotone, Illinois. Before being elected to the Illinois House, he served as Deputy District Administrator for Congressman Jesse L. Jackson, Jr.

William "Will" Davis

James T. Meeks

James T. Meeks, 2003–Present

The Reverend Senator James T. Meeks, born on August 4, 1956, was elected to the Illinois Senate in 2003. He is the first elected official elected as an Independent to the Illinois Senate. He defeated former Senator and now Mayor of Dolton William Shaw from the far South Side and southern suburbs. He was swept into office following a successful 1998 campaign to close 26 liquor stores in the Roseland neighborhood. It was that campaign that convinced Meeks to run as an independent against William Shaw for the state Senate seat in 2002.

He is the executive vice president for the Rainbow/PUSH Coalition. Meeks sponsored legislation to increase the income tax from 3 percent to 5 percent to fund education. Meeks pastors a $40 million church facility, the House of Hope, with seating for up to 12,000 in the Roseland community.

Meeks earned his Bachelor's Degree in religion and philosophy from Bishop College, in Dallas, Texas.

Chapter Four

Institutionalization of Black Political Power

ILLINOIS LEGISLATIVE BLACK CAUCUS, 1966–PRESENT

In an attempt to organize and institutionalize African-American lawmakers so that they would become a force to deal with in the Illinois General Assembly, in 1966, the late Representatives Harold Washington, Louis A.H. Caldwell, Otis Collins, and Calvin Smith formed a study group to examine issues affecting African-Americans in Illinois and to explore ways to address those critical issues. They realized that by capitalizing on the strengths of individual group members, much could be accomplished. The study group subsequently grew to include the late Senators Richard H. Newhouse, Charles Chew, Jr, and Kenneth Hall of East St. Louis. Former Representative Raymond Ewell was also part of the group. The study group became a formalized entity in 1968 as the Illinois Legislative Black Caucus (ILBC). The ILBC has represented the interests of Illinois citizens in numerous ways since its inception. There are now 28 who make-up the ILBC. They represent the most northern part of Illinois to the most southern part of the state.

Since the inception of the ILBC, its members have gone on to achieve great heights. As mentioned previously, Carol Moseley Braun and Senator Barack Obama have gone on to the U.S. Senate. Carol Braun became the first African-American to be elected Cook County's Recorder of Deeds, followed by Representative Eugene Moore. Representative Jesse White became Illinois' first African–American Secretary of State. Representative Harold Washington was elected as the first African-American Mayor for the City of Chicago. Senator William Shaw became Dolton, Illinois first African-American mayor.

In order to further institutionalize the ILBC, the group purchased its first home in Springfield in 2004, which was essential to stabilize the base for the

First Legislative Black Caucus Members

ILBC and maintain the official records of the ILBC. In January 2005, the
ILBC published its first African-American History Calendar. This initiative
was the vision of Representative Karen Yarbrough from Maywood, Illinois.
Because of the important role that Illinois African American legislators play
in public policy making, The HistoryMakers, founded by Julianne Richard-
son, has completed a comprehensive oral history on these great men and
women. The author has done a permanent photographic history of these
statesmen housed in Chicago State University new Academic Library in the
Legislative Assembly Room. The archives of some of these distinguished legislators are now housed at Chicago State University.

CONCLUSION

In Illinois, African-American state lawmakers have accomplished so much
during their service in the Illinois General Assembly since 1877 to the present. These men and women have come from myriad of backgrounds. They
have been and are medical doctors, pharmacists, dentists, lawyers, business-
men and women, ministers, writers, full-time elected officials and they come
from many other different professions. Their road to the state house has been
from serving in previous elected offices, heavy involvement in their respective communities and serving as public servants in different levels of local,

state and federal government. During the early part of the 20th century, many of them migrated from the south to the north in pursuit of better opportunities and a desire to escape Jim Croyism during the early 1900's and mid 1900's. Their accomplishments are noteworthy and deserve to be known by historians, students, scholars and the general public. Their accomplishments include sponsoring significant legislation such as the Illinois Abandoned Newborn Infant Protection Act, the Judicial Sub-District, increasing school funding, prohibition of racial profile, establishing The Human Rights Commission, promoting open housing legislation, senior advocacy laws, Voting Rights Act, the ERA Amendment, the Illinois Lottery, and advocating for minority contractors on state construction projects and other major laws. Not only have African-Americans benefited from their political vision but the general citizenry, women, children, gays, Hispanic, Latinos, and senior citizens throughout the State of Illinois and nationally have benefited significantly by their tireless efforts and commitment. They represent diverse constituents from the northern part of Illinois to the southern part of Illinois. This research is a compilation of their history.

References

Barnes, E. (September 2004). Former Member of the Illinois House of Representatives. Personal Interview.

———. (February, 2005). Former Member of the Illinois House of Representative. Personal Interview.

Benderoff, E. (July 6, 2007). High-speed internet hits home: African-Americans' usage is up sharply since '05 study says. *Chicago Tribune.* Business, Section 3, 1.

Biography for Jesse White Secretary of State. www.sos.state.il.us/biography.html. October 2003.

Black, L. (August 9, 2006). Safe-haven laws give babies a 2nd chance. *Chicago Tribune.* Metro. 1.

Black, Jr. T. D. (2003). *Bridges of Memory: Chicago's First Wave of Black Migration.* Northwestern University Press. Evanston, Illinois.

Braun-Moseley, B. "Biographical Information. www.bioguide.congress.gov/scripts/diodisplay.

Brown, M. (April 27, 2005). Racial Profiling Hot Topic at Northwestern Conference. *Chicago Defender,* 6.

Cecil A. Partee: Breaking Barriers in State and Local Government. Black History in Cook County. www.CecilA.Partee

Chase, J. & M. D. (November 3, 2004). Obama Scores a Record Landslide. *Chicago Tribune.* November 3, 2004. Section 1, p. 1 and 23 (backpage).

Clayborne, Jr. James F. State Senator–57th District. (October 11, 2005). Biographical Summary.

Collins, Annettzee. State Representative. (July 27, 2005). Telephone Interview.

Colvin, Marlow H. State Representative–33rd District. Biographical Information. (October 2005).

Constance A. "Connie" Howard. State Representative–34th District. Biographical Information. (July 2003).

———. "Connie" Howard. State Representative–34th District. Personal Interview. March 18, 2005.

Davis, Monique. State Representative–27th District. Biographical Information. (August 31, 2005).

Davis, William. State Representative–39th District. Biographical Information. (July 22, 2005).

Dunkin, Kenneth. State Representative 5th District. (July 19, 2005). Biogarphy.

Eckman, K. (May 20-22, 2005). State Debates Raising Adulthood to 18. *Chicago Defender.* 4.

Eddie Washington. (11/09/04). 60th District Representative. www.eddiewashington .com/abouteddie.html.

Eddie Washington revised biographical profile. (February 2005). 60th District Representative.

Emil Jones, Jr. Illinois State Senate President, Chicago. 14th District. www.senatedem .state.il.us.

Facts About Harold Washington: 42nd Mayor of Chicago. Biographical Information. www.chipublib.org/001hwlc/spehwpathfinder.htm'.

Fleming, T. (December 9, 1998). "Herbert Hoover Black Republicans: Reflections on Black History." *The Free Press.*

Flowers, Mary E. (July 6, 2005). Biographical Profile.

Graham, Deborah L. (October 21, 2005). 78th District. Biographical Information.

Guinane, P. (January 2005). Briefly. *Illinois Issues.* 8-12.

Harold Washington: Chicago Politician. www.lib.niu/ipo/ihy940472.ht .

Harris, K. M. "Generations of Pride: African American Timeline: A Selected Chronolog; .

Heinzmann, D. (June 18, 2005). Study Finds High Black Profiling: Crackdown skews numbers, Cline says. *Chicago Tribune.* Section 2, p. 18.

Hendon, Ricky R. Assistant Majority Leader/5th District. Telephone Interview. June 22, 2005.

Higher Education: Why It Matters. (November 9, 2005). Speakers. Pamphlet.

Hornsby, Jr. A. (2005). *A Companion to African-American History.* Blackwell Publishing. Malden, MA.

House Member Convicted. (January 2006). *Illinois Issues.* 32.

Hunter, Mattie. State Senator–3. (October 11, 2005). Biographical Summary

Illinois Blue Book–1959–1960. Edited by Illinois Secretary of State Charles F. Carpentier.

Illinois Blue Book–1979–1980. Edited by Illinois Secretary of State Alan J. Dixon.

Illinois Blue Book–1987–1988. Edited by Illinois Secretary of State Jim Edgar.

Illinois Blue Book–1991–1992. Edited by Illinois Secretary of State George H. Ryan.

Illinois Blue Book–1993–2004. Edited by Illinois Secretary of State George H. Ryan.

Illinois Blue Book–2003–2004. Edited by Illinois Secretary of State Jesse White.

Illinois General Assembly Legislative Synopsis and Digest. State of Illinois. (1921–1988).

Illinois House Democrats. (2001). Representative Chuck Jefferson. www.housedem .state.il.us/members/jeffersc .

Illinois House Journal. (1959). Legislative Reference Bureau.

Illinois Legislative Black Caucus 2005 Directory.

Illinois Legislative Black Caucus 1994-95. Members–Committee Assignments–Staff Contacts–4th Annual Issues Conference. Pamphlet. State of Illinois–May 1994.

Jarrett, V. (March 6, 1992). Voters Oust Two Who Gains for Constituents. *Sun Times.* 6.

Jefferson, Charles. Representative for the 67th Legislative District. January 24, 2005. Telephone Interview.

Joens, D. (2001, Summer) . John W.E. Thomas and the election of the first African American to the Illinois House of Representatives. *Journal of the Illinois State Historical Society.* 94. 200.

Johnson, Glen. Retired Cook County Judge. Telephone Interview. November 30, 2004.

Johnson, P. K. (November 11, 2004). Men of the Year. Essence. 159–172.

Jones, P. Silent Films Reflected, Influenced Black Society in the 1900's, Author Says. (July 28, 2005). Chicago Tribune. Section 5, p. 1.

Jones, Emil. "Moments to the Decision". Guest Lecturer. Chicago State University. May 4, 2007. Legislative Assembly Room.

———. (January 16, 2005). President of the Illinois State Senate. Personal Interview.

Kelly, Robin L. Representative for the 38th District. Biography. August 24, 2005. Know Your African-American State Legislator: Illinois Legislative Black Caucus. (May 2002). Pamphlet.

Kenney, D. & Hartley R. (2003). *An Uncertain Tradition: U.S. Senators from Illinois.* 1818–2003. Southern Illinois University Press. Carbondale, Illinois.

Lannan, M.S. (December 7, 2004). Obama Named to Key Panels. *Chicago Tribune.* Metro, p. 3.

Legislative Reference Unit First Reading. (November 2006). Dems Gain More Seats in General Assembly. Illinois General Assembly Legislative Research Unit.

Legislative Synopsis and Digest. (1955). Secretary of State.

Legislative Synopsis and Digest. (June 29, 1957). Secretary of State.

Legislative Synopsis and Digest. (January 9, 1973). Legislative Reference Bureau.

Legislative Synopsis and Digest. (January 12, 1977). Legislative Reference Bureau.

Legislative Synopsis and Digest. (January 30, 1978). Legislative Reference Bureau.

Legislative Synopsis and Digest. (March 30, 1989). Legislative Reference Bureau.

Lightford, Kimberly. (July 2005). Illinois State Senate 4th District Biography.

Miller, David. (July 10, 2006). Biography.

Nauer, K. (October 1990). Ten Worst Legislators. *Chicago Magazine.* 154-181.

Obama's Record in the Illinois Senate. (July 30, 2007). *The New York Times.* Section 1. p. 1.

Olszewski, L. (July 28, 2006). Meeks to hit street for better teachers *Chicago Tribune.* Metro, p. 3.

Owens, J. (February 25, 2005). African-American Clergy Becoming More Visible in Elected Offices. *Chicago Tribune.* Tempo, p. 2.

Palmer, Alice. (May 9, 2005). Former State Senator. Personal Interview.

Parsons, C., R. and S. Wescott. (September 19, 2004). Wheeler-dealer with a cause. *Chicago Tribune Magazine.* p. 13.

Pensoneau, T. (2006). *Power House: Arrington from Illinois.* Heritage Special Edition. Baltimore, Maryland.

Pioneers in the Struggle: The History of African Americans in the Illinois General Assembly, 1877-2001. (2001-2002). Videocassette/CD-ROM. The History Makers.

Pride, K. E. (October 10, 2005). Deborah Sawyer, founder and CEO, Environmental Design International Inc.: African American Firms Awarded Major Contracts on Dan Ryan. *Chicago Defender.* P. 3.

Profile E.M. Barnes & Associates. February 2005.

Rado, D. & Little D. (December 20, 2004). School District Spending Gap Widest in Years. *Chicago Tribune.* Section 1, pp. 1 & 16.

Reed, C. R. (2005). *Black Chicago's First Century: Volume I, 1833–1900.* University of Missouri Press: Columbia and London.

Richard J. Newhouse papers (manuscript). 1966–1989. Chicago Historical Society Research Center.

Schomburg Center for Research in Black Culture. The New York Public Library. An African-American Desk Reference. The Ultimate Source for Essential Information About History, Culture, and Contemporary Life. (1999). The Stonesong Press, Inc. The New York Public Library.

Senator Margaret Smith Capitol Report. 12 District Senator. August 1986.

Share the Vision Reception at Montay College Honoring The Honorable Cecil A. Partee. (June 17, 1994). Video Tape.

Sherman, P. (December 4, 2003). Mr. Jones Delivers. *Illinois Times* p. 1-9.

Singh, S.D. (February 7, 2005). City Schools Look to Fix Funding Gap. *Crain's* . 3

Slife, E. (April 6, 2005). House Bill Allows Suing of Pimps. *Chicago Tribune.* Section 2. p. 7.

Spear, A.K. (1967). *Black Chicago: The Making of a Negro Ghetto–1890–1920.* University of Chicago Press.

Starks, R. T. (June 21–27, 2001). State Rep. Connie Howard: A Powerhouse in the State House. Indigo.

———. (November 3–9, 2005). The Senator from Hyde Park. *Indigo.* 6.

State to Create Agency for Young Inmates. (November 5, 2005). *Chicago Tribune.* Metro and State. Section 1. 15.

State Rep. Louvana "Lou" Jones Biography-26th District.

Senate Resolution. SR0263 90th General Assembly. www.legis.state.il.u .

Senator Donne E. Trotter Biographical Profile. (2005).

"The New Negro." American Social History Project–Up South Video. www.ashp .cuny.edu/video/upy.html.

The Illinois Legislative Black Caucus 2nd Annual African-American Issues Conference. (1993). Pamphlet.

Three Decades of Public Affairs Journalism- Retrospective. (October 2004). *Illinois Issues.* 32.

Tribute to a Great Leader: Cecil A. Partee (House of Representatives–August 17, 1994). HR 8508.

Turner, Arthur. (July 10, 2006). Biography.

VanDyke-Brown, B. (2002). *Almanac of Illinois Politics–2002.* The Institute for Public Affairs. University of Illinois at Springfield. Springfield, Illinois. www.state.il .us/cou .

White, Jesse. (March 13, 2006). Illinois Secretary of State. Interview.

Washington, Eddie. (September 25, 2004). Member of the Illinois House of Representatives–District 60. Interview.

———. (July 5, 2005). Correspondence received from Representative Eddie Washington.

Wills, C. (May 18, 2005). Advocates say 'Safe Haven' Law Working, Should be Permanent. *Chicago Defender.* 4.

———. (January 10, 2005). Lawmakers Return to End Old Session, Launch New One. *Chicago Defender.* 2.

Williams, Paul. (September 2004). Former Member of the Illinois House of Representatives. Interview.

Yarbrough, Karen. (July 2006). Biography.

———. (December 2006). All in the Family. *State Legislatures.*

Zeleny, J. (June 26, 2007). Obama, In New TV Ads, Focues on His Pre-Senate Years. The New York Times. A16.

Index

www.ingramcontent.com/pod-product-compliance
Lightning Source LLC
Chambersburg PA
CBHW020358270326
41926CB00007B/488